THE STRANGE CASE OF DR JEKYLL & MR HYDE

by Robert Louis Stevenson

Adapted by Nick Lane

Playdead Press

Published by Playdead Press 2012

A CIP catalogue record for this book is available from the British Library.

ISBN 978-0-9572859-3-4

Playdead Press
www.playdeadpress.com

Nick Lane is a playwright and director as well as the Literary Manager of Hull Truck Theatre. His original plays include: Me and Me Dad, My Favourite Summer, Blue Cross Xmas, The Derby McQueen Affair, Housebound and Seconds Out. His literary adaptations include: Frankenstein, Lady Chatterley's Lover, Moby Dick (with John Godber) and 1984. He has also written and directed a number of original children's shows and adaptations including: 'Twas The Night Before Christmas, When Santa Got Stuck in the Fridge, The Kit Basket & Other Stories, Pinocchio, A Christmas Carol, The Elves & the Shoemaker and Hansel & Gretel. He lives in Doncaster, supports Doncaster Rovers and if he's honest could do with not eating burgers or noodles for a bit.

For Button and Chirp

This production was commissioned by Hull Truck Theatre Company for performance through autumn 2012. The cast (in order of character appearance) was as follows:

Eleanor Lanyon, an adventuress	Joanna Miller
Gabriel John Utterson, a lawyer	John Gully
Dr. Henry Jekyll, a scientist	James Weaver
Richard Enfield, a socialite	John Gully
Molly, a servant in Enfield's employ	Joanna Miller
Doctor, a doctor	James Weaver
Mother, a stricken child's mother	Joanna Miller
Father, a stricken child's father	James Weaver
Mr. Edward Hyde, a beast	James Weaver
Miss Bradshaw, Jekyll's servant	Joanna Miller
Dr. Hastings Lanyon, a colleague	John Gully/ James Weaver
Annie, a prostitute	Joanna Miller
Poole, a servant in Jekyll's employ	James Weaver
Sir Denvers Carew, a politician	John Gully
Inspector Newcomen, a detective	James Weaver

Director Nick Lane.

All original music was written, performed and recorded by Tristan Parkes. The set & lighting was designed by Graham Kirk. All costumes were designed by Sian Thomas.

Please note this publication may differ slightly to the final performance.

THE STRANGE CASE OF DR JEKYLL & MR HYDE

by Robert Louis Stevenson
Adapted by Nick Lane

"Science does not make it impossible to believe in God. It just makes it possible to not believe in God."
Steven Weinberg

"Two is a number. It is, in fact, the number two."
Dr. Darren Haggerston, PhD.

ACT ONE. The stage is an abstract representation of a Victorian music hall space, scratched wood floors and mildewed red curtains; tarnished conch lights on the forestage. There are three chairs, set diagonally across the space, upstage right, stage centre and downstage left. At the back in either corner are packing crates, and on one side a table, upended. There is a hat-and-coat stand in the space upstage left; a silk scarf amongst other things draped around it. Upstage right, initially covered by a dirt-caked drop-cloth is a blackboard. Pre-set is faint light as if from a window. Music plays as the audience enter. At front of house clearance, house lights fade and the music changes. ***ELEANOR****, an attractive woman in her late twenties or early thirties, enters wearing appropriate attire. She walks across the space and stands in front of the chair downstage. Next,* ***UTTERSON*** *enters; a rumpled, careworn figure in his early to mid-forties. He stands at the chair upstage. Finally,* ***JEKYLL*** *enters. He is a handsome, serious-looking man in his early to mid-forties. He walks with the aid of a cane, and takes his position centre. At present they are all wearing identical classic Devil masks and stare out. There is a particular point in the music at which first* ***UTTERSON****, then* ***JEKYLL*** *and finally* ***ELEANOR*** *take off their masks, at which signal the lights fade up slightly and the actors address the audience with the same line,* ***JEKYLL*** *starting, then* ***UTTERSON*** *and finally* ***ELEANOR****. It is a spoken round, recited only once and picking up after the word 'wisdom.'*

JEKYLL *(To audience)* Alas. How terrible is wisdom when it brings no profit to the wise. This I knew well, but had forgotten it, else I would not have come here.

UTTERSON *(To audience)* Alas. How terrible is wisdom when it brings no profit to the wise. This I knew well, but had forgotten it, else I would not have come here.

ELEANOR *(To audience)* Alas. How terrible is wisdom when it brings no profit to the wise. This I knew well, but had forgotten it, else I would not have come here.

*Slowly **ELEANOR** and **UTTERSON** turn their heads to favour **JEKYLL**.*

JEKYLL *(To audience)* What is a man? By what do we measure pre-eminence; our physical experiences, or the life of the mind?

UTTERSON *(To audience)* I am of no importance. You will not have heard of me. When I die it will be as if I had never existed.

JEKYLL *(To audience)* What is it that makes us matter?

ELEANOR *(To audience)* The only man that ever mattered to me; the only man I truly, truly loved... I gave this mask.

UTTERSON *(To audience)* This mask I found on my good friend. And he was important. You will have heard of him.

ELEANOR *(To audience)* My name is Eleanor Lanyon.

UTTERSON *(To audience)* I am Gabriel John Utterson.

As ***JEKYLL*** *speaks his name,* ***UTTERSON*** *and* ***ELEANOR*** *whisper 'Edward Hyde.'*

JEKYLL *(To audience)* My name is Henry Jekyll.

JEKYLL *has to repeat himself – is he hearing things, is it a guilty conscience? This time* ***UTTERSON*** *and* ***ELEANOR*** *are a little louder with the name 'Edward Hyde.'*

My name is Henry Jekyll.

Last time; ***JEKYLL*** *more insistent – he definitely heard it that time. Both times,* ***UTTERSON*** *and* ***ELEANOR*** *say 'Edward Hyde' over* ***JEKYLL****'s own.*

Henry Jekyll! My name… is Henry Jekyll!

Recorded scream; sting of music and activity. ***ELEANOR*** *moves her chair so that it is next to* ***JEKYLL****'s centre-stage, then she and* ***JEKYLL*** *head upstage, placing their masks in one of the upstage left cases.* ***UTTERSON*** *places his mask in a case upstage right before moving his chair to the other side of* ***JEKYLL****'s and standing in front of it.*

UTTERSON *(To audience)* The case of Dr. Henry Jekyll and Mr. Edward Hyde began on a crisp winter morning in 1895. It was my habit at that time to take walks on a Sunday with friend, client – I am a lawyer by profession – and socialite, Richard Enfield.

***ELEANOR** crosses to **UTTERSON** with the silk scarf from the hat-stand. She has briefly become **MOLLY**, a servant. She puts the scarf over his shoulders as he continues to address the audience.*

Now Enfield was heavier set than I, and from the North of England. He would wear a scarf of this type, and was like to keep a pipe burning, especially on cold days, such as it was.

He removes a pipe from his pocket and sticks it in the corner of his mouth, as if taking a tug on it.

He had a deep voice and an eye for the fairer sex. None of his housemaids were safe from the devil...

*He looks at **MOLLY** suddenly.*

*(As **ENFIELD**, suddenly)* My, you're a pretty thing; how long have I been employing you?

MOLLY Excuse me, sir?

UTTERSON *(As* ***ENFIELD****)* No, I don't think I will, unless you give me a name… or a favour.

He winks.

MOLLY Oh!

UTTERSON *is himself once more.* ***MOLLY*** *curtseys, moves upstage, turns and is* ***ELEANOR*** *again.*

UTTERSON *(To audience)* Quite the man about town is Richard Enfield. And though we rarely spoke on our Sunday strolls, for my part, I looked forward to them immensely.

UTTERSON *perches on the edge of one of the chairs.*

(To audience) On the Sunday in question we happened to stop in a park opposite a particular building as Enfield lit his pipe –

UTTERSON *pretends to draw on the pipe.*

– then gestured with it. *(As* ***ENFIELD****)* "You see that door over there?" he said. I nodded. *(As* ***ENFIELD****)* "It is connected in my mind with a very odd story…"

Lights.

ENFIELD *(To audience)* It was three o'clock of a black winter morning, I was coming back from… some place or another, and my way lay through a part of town where there was nothing to be seen but lamps. I'd walked in silence for quite some time, when all at once, I saw two figures –

There is the sound of footfall with slight echo.

– one, a girl of maybe eight or ten; what she was doing out at that hour God alone can tell, but she was running flat out westward… eastward came the other, a gentleman stamping along at a good pace. Naturally they ran into one another at the corner… and then came the horrible part, for the man, with no change of speed or direction, and being the heavier of the two, knocked the girl to the ground… then proceeded to trample on her stricken body.

***ELEANOR** screams.*

It sounds less than it was, but I swear to you, had you been there… he wasn't like a man. He was like a Juggernaut. Well sir, I caught up with the fellow and brought him back to where the child lay screaming and crying. By now, there was quite a group; people woken from their rest by the noise, other passers-by, the girl's parents, and – what was most fortunate – a doctor.

Upstage, ***JEKYLL*** *becomes the voice of the* ***DOCTOR****.*

DOCTOR The child's all right; more shaken up than anything else.

There is the sound of an angry mob low in the mix, building through the next section.

ENFIELD *(To audience)* The crowd quickly surrounded the aggressor...

ELEANOR *gives voice to the* ***MOTHER****.*

MOTHER What were you thinking of, you monster? My little girl! My little girl!

JEKYLL *is now the* ***FATHER****.*

FATHER You could have killed her; don't you see that?

MOTHER You're evil.

ENFIELD A madman.

DOCTOR What's your name, sir?

MOTHER Evil!

ENFIELD Hurting an innocent child!

FATHER We'll make such a scandal of this, your name will stink from one end of London to the other!

This next section speeds up, with the sounds of the voices.

MOTHER Evil!
DOCTOR Name, sir!
MOTHER Monster!
ENFIELD Madman!
MOTHER Evil!
DOCTOR Name, sir!
MOTHER Monster!
FATHER Scandal!

Then, at once, the sound stops.

ENFIELD *(To audience)* Before I knew it, we were a mob. All of us ready to kill for the sake of a child's cuts and bruises. The men had to hold the women back; they were as wild as harpies. Even the doctor, who seemed a most conservative fellow, appeared sick with desire to do the man harm. I was no different. My nails dug into my palms enough to draw blood. I had almost lost all reason. And there, at the centre, stood the man, his face fearful, but also with a kind of black, sneering coolness.

***JEKYLL** provides the voice of **HYDE**.*

HYDE If you want to make something of it –

ENFIELD *(To audience)* He said –

HYDE – I am helpless. But I would rather not cause a scene. Name your price.

ENFIELD *(To audience)* Name your price? Did you ever hear the like?

MOTHER A hundred pounds!

ENFIELD *(To audience)* The girl's mother called out. And before I knew it, I was adding my consent. 'A hundred! Yes!'

MOTHER Pay it!

ENFIELD Pay it now!

HYDE Follow me –

ENFIELD *(To audience)* – said the villain, and every one of us followed him to this very door. He produced a key, went inside, then returned with ten pounds in gold, and a cheque for the balance, signed with a name I won't mention, save to say that you know the gentleman. After that… well, too many questions lead to trouble, as you know, so I asked nothing more than the villain's identity, one Edward Hyde. But ever since that night, the sight of that door… fair turns my stomach.

*Lights return to the previous state. Music plays under the following; a slightly sinister refrain. **UTTERSON** takes off* *the scarf. He is himself once more, and moves one of the chairs so it is at an angle from the other two.*

(As ***UTTERSON****; to audience)* The door in question is blistered and distained, equipped with neither bell nor knocker, and attached to the blackened outer wall of a building in West London, on a street close to a court wherein sits the residence of my good friend, Dr. Jekyll. It was this last fact that troubled me most as I left Enfield that winter morning. It brought to mind a conversation that had taken place several months earlier…

JEKYLL *moves into the scene, walking stiffly and leaning on the cane. Lights.*

JEKYLL My dear Utterson! How good of you to come! *(Calling)* Miss Bradshaw?

JEKYLL *struggles to ease himself into the 'two seater' as* ***UTTERSON*** *continues.*

UTTERSON *(To audience)* For as long as I had known him, Dr. Jekyll had always struggled physically – suffering colds and blood-fevers as well as whatever ailment necessitated the use of a cane. Familiarity and fondness led me to call him Harry; in return, he alone would address me by my middle name…

JEKYLL Sit, John; sit. I have no patients for the rest of the day, so…

UTTERSON I can't stay long, honestly. Much as I would like to.

***BRADSHAW**, a pretty young servant girl (played by **ELEANOR**) enters and curtseys.*

JEKYLL Ah, Miss Bradshaw. Do we have any Turkish coffee?

BRADSHAW I don't know sir. I can ask. I don't drink it myself, sir. Awful stuff. Cook made me try some; tasted like soil.

JEKYLL *(Smiling)* It's not to everyone's taste, I agree. Nevertheless, could you prepare a pot?

BRADSHAW Very good, sir.

She curtseys and exits. A beat.

JEKYLL Well! To business. I have made a change to my Will.

UTTERSON Oh?

JEKYLL I see you are displeased.

UTTERSON I think surprise more than displeasure is to the fore.

JEKYLL Because I didn't engage your services?

UTTERSON No…

A beat. ***UTTERSON*** *smiles.*

UTTERSON Perhaps.

JEKYLL Don't worry. I have not procured myself another lawyer; you are my man. I did this by myself.

JEKYLL *takes a document from the table and hands it to* ***UTTERSON.***

UTTERSON I wish you hadn't.

JEKYLL It's all legal.

UTTERSON It's not the legality; it's your handwriting. The slopes, the loops… you doctors are all alike. *(**UTTERSON** opens the document; reads from it)* "I, Henry Jekyll, M.D., D.C.L., L.L.D., F.R.S., etc." I've got a migraine already.

JEKYLL Don't mock.

UTTERSON *(Reading)* "Declare, upon the occasion of my death, that all my possessions pass into the hands of my friend and benefactor… Edward Hyde."

A beat. ***UTTERSON*** *looks at* ***JEKYLL.***

JEKYLL Read on.

UTTERSON, *concerned, turns back to the Will.*

UTTERSON *(Reading)* "... and further, that in the case of my disappearance or unexplained absence for any period exceeding three calendar months, the said Edward Hyde should step into my shoes without further delay and free from any burden or obligation beyond the payment of a few small sums to the members of the household currently under employ."

A beat. ***JEKYLL****, looking over his shoulder, completes the reading.*

JEKYLL *(Reading)* "Here witness my hand, this fourteenth day of August, 1895."

JEKYLL *takes a fountain pen, leans over* ***UTTERSON*** *and signs the Will, then returns to his seat.*

The look on your face is exactly why I needed to draw the Will alone.

UTTERSON I can't countenance this.

JEKYLL Too late. There it is.

UTTERSON Hyde.

JEKYLL Yes.

UTTERSON Edward Hyde?

JEKYLL *nods.*

Need I ask...?

***JEKYLL** continues to smile.*

Have I met him?

***JEKYLL** shakes his head.*

Then who is he? A long-lost family friend, recently returned from the continent? Tell me that.

JEKYLL You'll accept that?

UTTERSON No, but it would make it easier to understand.

JEKYLL All you need to know is that he is a gentleman in whom I have the utmost trust.

UTTERSON I hope so, Harry. This document; it is unconventional to say the least.

JEKYLL The very least.

*A beat. **JEKYLL** smiles.*

My dear friend, I assure you, I did not write this Will under duress, it is my desire and mine alone that I should leave my fortune to Mr. Hyde. That is all you need to know.

***UTTERSON** stands.*

Now, are you sure you won't stay? For coffee, at least.

UTTERSON I have other business in town...

A beat.

JEKYLL Something else...?

UTTERSON Do not take this the wrong way...

JEKYLL You'd better say whatever 'this' is, and I'll judge which way to take it.

UTTERSON Harry, I've known you for almost fifteen years...

JEKYLL Thirteen; I've been counting.

UTTERSON You helped me move my sister into a more secure institution; you came to my mother's funeral... then when Elizabeth's madness took its toll, you came to hers too...

JEKYLL I know. I'm a jinx.

UTTERSON I've never heard you even mention this Hyde fellow.

JEKYLL *(Mock relief)* Oh! For a second there, I thought you were angling for an inheritance.

UTTERSON Don't be ridiculous. I'm fine, financially; though... did you mention any of this to Hastings at all?

*Music plays very faintly under – 'Danse Macabre' by Saint-Saens. **JEKYLL** is lost in thought.*

Harry?

JEKYLL Sorry?
UTTERSON Hastie? Have you spoken with him?
JEKYLL Oh; I...
UTTERSON Are you all right?

*From across the back, in an outfit representing a Victorian version of the Devil, complete with cloak and mask, **ELEANOR** enters and dances round the pair of them. It is all in **JEKYLL**'s head.*

JEKYLL Yes. Yes, I... I'm fine.
UTTERSON Do you need to sit down?
JEKYLL I probably need to eat.
UTTERSON Then I won't keep you.

They shake hands.

I'll see you very soon.

JEKYLL *(Trying to keep it together)* I do hope so, John.

***UTTERSON** exits. **JEKYLL** sits down heavily, wincing with pain and mopping his brow with a handkerchief. As he addresses the audience, **ELEANOR** dances the chairs so they are evenly spaced across the centre-line, like a row of theatre seats, before exiting.*

(To audience) On October the twentieth, 1884, I was studying Medicine at Bart's. And I was angry. My friend and fellow student, Hastings Lanyon had asked me, with typical exuberance, to join him at Wilton's Music Hall in Spitalfields for the evening.

Lights; we are in a variety theatre. Audience sounds mixed in with the Saint-Saens.

I was in no mood to entertain such a request, but as he had become in all but name my assistant, to refuse seemed uncommonly rude. I arrived early. He was late… as usual…

***UTTERSON** enters, now wearing a different jacket and with a pair of spectacles on his nose, as **LANYON**. He edges along the row of seats and joins **JEKYLL**. They stare out into the audience as if watching a performance.*

LANYON Before you say anything, don't.
JEKYLL I wasn't going to.

A beat.

LANYON Sorry.

JEKYLL No; don't worry – I'm only on the verge of the single-most important discovery in our field. It can wait.

LANYON Splendid.

JEKYLL I was being sarcastic.

LANYON I know.

He gestures out front. Behind them in a spot, we see ***ELEANOR*** *dancing, beckoning, turning… she is Mephistopheles. This is stylised; a slow-motion effect.*

Here she comes; here she comes.

JEKYLL If I'm right, and I can prove it, I will be the English Charcot.

LANYON I couldn't believe it was a girl at first; the costume!

JEKYLL Actually, the French may start referring to Charcot as their Jekyll.

LANYON She sings in the second half; you should hear her voice!

JEKYLL I need a little more time in the lab… some peace and quiet…

LANYON I've been to every performance.

JEKYLL And more subjects, obviously.

A beat.

LANYON You do know we're at a theatre, don't you?

JEKYLL What?

LANYON You're supposed to be enjoying yourself.

JEKYLL How?

***LANYON** indicates in front of him at the 'stage.' **JEKYLL** fails to be impressed.*

LANYON It's dance; the story of Faust. He sells his soul to Mephistopheles in return for – (knowledge and power)

JEKYLL I know the story.

LANYON Did you also know I invited you here to meet my future wife?

JEKYLL I beg your pardon?

LANYON I proposed this afternoon, old boy.

JEKYLL *(Preoccupied)* Well. Congratulations.

LANYON Isn't she perfect?

***JEKYLL** watches for a second.*

JEKYLL She's very nice. Strange face.

LANYON She's wearing a mask.

JEKYLL Of course she is. Of course she is. I swear this theory will – (secure my place amongst...)

LANYON Henry!

JEKYLL Sorry. Very good.

*The music finishes, and applause builds. **JEKYLL** joins in. **LANYON** stands, applauding wildly, whistling and cheering.*

***JEKYLL** feels obliged to stand too, which he does with some effort, by which time the applauding has finished and he wants to sit down. **ELEANOR** bows and exits. Lights up slightly.*

LANYON What are you doing?

JEKYLL Sitting.

LANYON No! Absolutely not! Come on!

JEKYLL Why?

LANYON Stage door. She said she'd see us at the interval.

JEKYLL Who did?

LANYON Just follow me...

***LANYON** takes the centre chair upstage and exits. **JEKYLL** turns to the audience.*

JEKYLL *(To audience)* I wasn't being deliberately obtuse; I had a lot on my mind. Lanyon knew I did too, which was what made the situation all the more enervating. Still, I played along for his sake, and waited as he went to fetch his 'Colleen...'

***JEKYLL** positions himself to the left of the stage left chair. **LANYON** enters, giggling, followed by **ELEANOR**, holding a bunch of flowers.*

LANYON Ah! There you are! Henry Jekyll...

***ELEANOR** emerges from the 'doorway.'*

…meet Eleanor O'Donnell, the Irish songbird… and my fiancée.

***JEKYLL** looks up at **ELEANOR**. He takes her hand as she offers it.*

ELEANOR Hastie's told me lots about you.

JEKYLL Indeed?

ELEANOR You're the smartest person he's ever met apparently.

JEKYLL I'm not the judge of who else he's met, but…

ELEANOR Oh! Modest too!

***JEKYLL** smiles thinly.*

JEKYLL It was a pleasure meeting you.

LANYON Are you leaving?

JEKYLL Yes.

LANYON Don't you want to hear her sing?

JEKYLL I've seen and heard enough, thank you.

LANYON But –

JEKYLL *(Quietly; to **LANYON**)* I'm sorry, Hastie, but your dalliance with an Irish toffer is not going to change the world. I am.

LANYON This isn't a dalliance, and Miss O'Donnell is no toffer.

ELEANOR I am Irish though.

LANYON My darling, there is no need to – (get involved in this sort of argument)

ELEANOR *(To **LANYON**)* It's fine, Hastie; it's fine. I can fight my own battles. *(To **JEKYLL**)* So what is going to change the world, Dr. Jekyll?

JEKYLL I doubt you'll understand.

ELEANOR I can try.

JEKYLL I am looking into the possibility of actively splitting the mind.

A beat.

ELEANOR For what purpose?

JEKYLL To seek out the root of what makes us who we are.

LANYON I believe my colleague is having a joke at our expense.

JEKYLL No joke, I assure you. If I can tap into the thinking mind, I should be able to examine, understand and cure all manner of disorders.

LANYON It isn't possible.

ELEANOR I'd like to see that.

JEKYLL I don't think you would.

ELEANOR Why not?

JEKYLL Because this kind of practice belongs in a world you do not and cannot inhabit.

LANYON I believe what Henry is saying is that the lab room at Bart's is not the place for a woman…

ELEANOR Hastie, I grew up around animals; there's not much I haven't seen.

A beat.

JEKYLL Why don't you come then?

LANYON Now, see here old boy…

ELEANOR Tonight?

JEKYLL *(Aping **ELEANOR**)* Why not?

LANYON Eleanor doesn't take her curtain call until well after ten.

JEKYLL I'll still be there.

***JEKYLL** smiles at **ELEANOR**, then exits. **LANYON** and **ELEANOR** look at one another.*

LANYON Well! I must apologise!

ELEANOR Trust me, I've had worse reviews than that.

LANYON You know I don't think that of you, don't you?

There is the sound of a handbell ringing.

Ah! Best get back to the auditorium.

ELEANOR Hastie, you've seen the show a dozen times…

LANYON And it's better every night. *(She smiles.)* We don't need to go to Bart's tonight if you'd rather not...

ELEANOR Oh, I wouldn't miss it for the world. After all, the good doctor's seen my dance; it's only fair I get to see his.

***LANYON** smiles, kisses **ELEANOR**'s hand and exits. **ELEANOR** moves the stage left chair back downstage to where it started as she addresses the audience.*

(To audience) As first impressions go, Henry Jekyll's was lasting for all the wrong reasons. He was curt, rude, and work-obsessed... yet for all that, I was excited riding in Hastie's carriage towards St. Bartholomew's.

***JEKYLL** enters and takes the table from the back, standing it upright in an upstage corner. He takes a number of phials, jars and flasks from the various cases and places them in front of him. He next pulls a cloth from the blackboard, revealing equations and symbols. He starts chalking additions to it.*

Upon arrival we walked hurriedly through corridors and classrooms, before arriving at a gas lit laboratory...

***JEKYLL** looks round.*

JEKYLL Where's Dr. Lanyon?

ELEANOR He ran into one of your colleagues – Dr. Stevens, I believe his name was. He'll be along directly.

JEKYLL Always late. Always.

***JEKYLL** takes from the floor a small crate. He places it on the table, then continues to set up.*

ELEANOR What's in there?

JEKYLL A rat.

ELEANOR What are you going to do with it?

JEKYLL Inject it with something, watch it and kill it.

ELEANOR *(Trying to make a joke)* In that order?

***JEKYLL** does not respond.*

Are you always this discourteous, Dr. Jekyll, or is it just towards members of the opposite sex?

*Again, **JEKYLL** pays little attention, noting things down, bringing out lab equipment etc.*

Perhaps it's me specifically you have difficulty with?

***JEKYLL** says nothing.*

You know, my father and two of my brothers all died of cholera when I was nine years old. My mother thought me too young to attend the funerals, and I was forced to spend those days alone in my room. I never felt so shut out in my life... until tonight.

***JEKYLL** looks her straight in the eye.*

JEKYLL I don't have difficulty with you.

*They look at one another. **LANYON** enters.*

Hastie! About time! I need a combination of potassium glutamate and lithium carbonate in an alcohol solution. Don't think; do it.

***LANYON** rolls his eyes and starts to mix compounds.*

Then, add bromide solution number one from that phial over there. All the measurements are marked on the sides of the relevant containers.

LANYON What in blazes are you doing?

JEKYLL Making history.

LANYON What?

JEKYLL Next; two drops of chloral hydrate. Come on; come on, before I forget it!

LANYON Isn't this written down anywhere?

JEKYLL Sort of. Not yet. My God, this… this is it! This could be it!

LANYON Where are you – (getting this from?)

ELEANOR What's going on?

JEKYLL I'm stimulating astrocytes.

LANYON Why?

JEKYLL Wrong question.

ELEANOR What are astrocytes?

JEKYLL A form of glial cell.

ELEANOR That doesn't really help me.

LANYON Glial is from the Greek for glue. Glial cells hold the neurons in the brain in place; help them do their job by –

JEKYLL *(Suddenly)* No! No; that's sodium triphosphate! I already tried that; it doesn't work. Oh, let me!

***JEKYLL** takes over mixing the chemicals. **LANYON** picks up where he left off.*

LANYON …glial cells provide support, insulation and nutrients for the neurons in the brain as they fire.

JEKYLL And that's all they do, is it?

LANYON Well, with respect, Cajal, Charcot, Golgi… none of them believe that – (glial cells do anything but provide padding for the neurons)

JEKYLL None of them are me.

LANYON Don't be preposterous.

JEKYLL This isn't preposterous. Think, man; ever since the connection was made between neurons in the sense organs and those up here, they're all anyone looks at. And yet they account for only 10% of the brain.

ELEANOR The rest are these astrocytes?

JEKYLL And other glial cells, but yes. They're all over the cerebral cortex.

***JEKYLL** is checking notes; flying round the space, absolutely possessed by it. In some small way, **ELEANOR** assists, though it is unspoken.*

LANYON That doesn't prove – (or disprove anything)

JEKYLL Neurons control motor function, yes; no-one's denying that. But who we are – why we think what we think, why we dream... our intelligence, our personality... what if that is down to the astrocytes?

***LANYON** is looking at the blackboard, trying to follow **JEKYLL's** fevered notes.*

LANYON This is beyond reason...

JEKYLL Just because neurons were found first, doesn't mean we should stop looking. If they fire like neurons, which I strongly suspect they will... then by actively stimulating – or preventing the stimulation of – astrocytes...

ELEANOR ...you can investigate the mind of a living being.

*A beat. **JEKYLL** looks up. **ELEANOR** is quicker on the uptake than **LANYON**.*

JEKYLL If you're at all interested I could give you a number of papers to read on the subject.

***LANYON** opens his mouth to speak on her behalf. She is in too quickly for him.*

ELEANOR I'd like that.

***LANYON** turns away from the blackboard.*

LANYON I take it you've done this before?

JEKYLL Variations, yes.

LANYON How many rats have you used?

JEKYLL Some. Why do you think I need you to get my test subjects for me? They won't give me any more. I have to steal them.

LANYON There is such a thing as the Cruelty to Animals Act...

JEKYLL I'm well aware of the law...

LANYON You just choose to ignore it?

JEKYLL No; I choose to see the greater good.

LANYON There is no greater good!

JEKYLL	Must we do this every time? Rats aren't people.
LANYON	Which makes it all right?
JEKYLL	Eleanor, if I may – you said your father died of cholera, yes?
ELEANOR	That's right.
JEKYLL	And if he could have lived to see you marry Hastie... see you bear children... how many rats would that be worth to you?
LANYON	This is in poor taste...
JEKYLL	*(To **LANYON**)* No no no no no; *(To **ELEANOR**)* How many? One? Ten? A hundred?

A beat.

ELEANOR	I couldn't count the number.
LANYON	That's a horrible over-simplification on your part, dear boy, not to mention hugely manipulative...
JEKYLL	Forget the question then. But remember the answer.

***JEKYLL** takes a syringe from one of the crates.*

Here; here...

He draws a little of the solution he has mixed into the syringe, and reaches into the box. There is the sound of a squeak, as if he has taken hold of the rat, then he clears air from the syringe.

The change should occur fairly rapidly...

ELEANOR What are you expecting to see?

JEKYLL There are certain function tests I can run once I get a subject that survives the initial phase. By monitoring stimulated and non-stimulated states we should be able to...

ELEANOR I'm with you.

LANYON And I'm not.

***JEKYLL** puts the syringe into the box. Another squeak.*

JEKYLL *(To **LANYON**)* What did Stevens want? I'm normally alone at night.

LANYON He came in for some equipment. He's volunteering on the Endymion.

ELEANOR The what?

LANYON It's a ship. One of two anchored in the Thames. On loan to the asylums board. For all the smallpox sufferers.

JEKYLL With all the gambling debts he's accrued, I suppose he's got to hide somewhere.

LANYON He's not hiding. He's helping.

JEKYLL Eight hundred stricken Londoners and Maxwell Stevens' ego. Let's hope the ships can take it.

LANYON He says they're expecting 40% mortality.

JEKYLL That few?

LANYON Better than some of the slum districts.

JEKYLL *(To **ELEANOR**)* Have you been vaccinated?

ELEANOR No.

JEKYLL We can do that while you're here.

LANYON *(Embarrassed; he should have thought of this)* Can we?

***JEKYLL** checks his pocket watch.*

JEKYLL Hastie, take the rat over to the maze, would you?

ELEANOR Is the vaccine not just for your staff?

JEKYLL No, there's simply not enough of the stuff – (to get it to everyone)

*As this conversation takes place, **LANYON** reaches into the box, inside of which is a sponge soaked in stage blood. There is a sting of music and a rat screech. **LANYON** squeezes the sponge to create a gush of blood, and cries out in pain, withdrawing his hand.*

LANYON Ah! Christ!

ELEANOR Are you all right?

LANYON It's bit through the tendon!

JEKYLL	Blast.
ELEANOR	What happened?
JEKYLL	Another schizoid embolism, by the looks. Damn it.
LANYON	Jesus! Jesus! Ah!
JEKYLL	I thought I had it; I…
LANYON	I've… never felt a bite like it…
JEKYLL	Perhaps… perhaps the addition of some form of protein… or…
ELEANOR	Hold still. Let me see.
JEKYLL	Maybe an opiate injected prior to the solution so as to… yes… might…

***JEKYLL** looks at **LANYON**'s hand.*

That'll need stitching.

ELEANOR	The rat's going mad.
LANYON	Be careful, old boy; it's – (got a jaw like a steel trap)

*But without waiting for the rest of **LANYON**'s warning, **JEKYLL** reaches into the box, this time bringing out a model rat, and swiftly, and in a matter-of-fact manner, he slams it down onto the edge of the table, breaking its neck. He then tosses it back into the box. Music. **LANYON** exits. **JEKYLL** starts to clear away the lab scene as **ELEANOR** addresses the audience.*

ELEANOR *(To audience)* In June of 1885, I became the wife of Hastings Lanyon, and moved from a rented room in Spitalfields to a house on Cavendish Square. I was comfortable; provided for... but Hastie's opinions on independence were traditional to say the least. He wasn't blind to my unrest – and he could see I wasn't happy running a house – but instead of intervening himself, he gave me leave to travel with Dr. Jekyll as he pursued his theories around the country...

We hear seagulls; shore wash. ***JEKYLL*** *approaches. Lights.*

This reminds me of Blacksod Bay back home.

JEKYLL The last train... we'd better...

A beat. They stare out together.

ELEANOR Did you get everything you needed?
JEKYLL They won't let me carry out formula tests, but the observation was useful.
ELEANOR Who is she?
JEKYLL Her name's Elizabeth. Elizabeth Utterson. She's the sister of a good friend.
ELEANOR What they're doing to her...

JEKYLL	It's barbaric. You recognised the apparatus?
ELEANOR	The Tranquiliser Chair, yes. From your man Rush. The American.
JEKYLL	Top of the class.
ELEANOR	Your work will change all that; why can't they see it?
JEKYLL	They will in time. I hope.

He steps towards her; winces.

ELEANOR	Are you...?
JEKYLL	Fine; it's... from time to time, I...
ELEANOR	Do you need to rest?
JEKYLL	Probably.

She takes his arm. He smiles. They look out together.

ELEANOR	You'd like Blacksod Bay. There's a house by the water's edge with a vaulted roof, and a set of steps leading down to the shore. Stones on the beach the colour of rust, and the air all clean and salty, just like here.
JEKYLL	Could you live there?
ELEANOR	One day, maybe. With the right man.

Pause. Tension.

It's hard to love anyone from a pedestal.

JEKYLL I see.

ELEANOR He allows me to indulge my 'little whim' by coming out with you...

JEKYLL Perhaps with time, he might...

A beat.

ELEANOR How many other hospitals can you try?

JEKYLL This was the last. If I can't test here I'll need to think of something a little more radical...

ELEANOR Maybe I could talk to them.

JEKYLL I doubt that would work.

ELEANOR *(Smiling)* I don't know. I can be quite persuasive...

A beat.

JEKYLL The train.

ELEANOR You head down. I'll catch you. Want to get my last breath of sea air...

***JEKYLL** starts to move upstage, then turns back and breathes **ELEANOR** in briefly. She smiles. She addresses the audience. **JEKYLL** reaches an upstage corner and turns to face her once more.*

(To audience) His passion, his absolute conviction... with Henry, I felt alive in a way that I couldn't anywhere else...

including the place I called home. But... as the years wore on and things changed, I found I lost the will to rail against my situation. And a cage is a cage, however gilded...

Music; a Christmas carol. Lights. ***UTTERSON*** *enters singing heartily.* ***ELEANOR*** *rearranges the chairs, singing along with him. She takes the dirty white sheet that had previously been covering the blackboard and throws it over the table and equipment.* ***UTTERSON*** *holds* ***LANYON's*** *spectacles and jacket and, in view of the audience, dresses* ***JEKYLL*** *as* ***LANYON.*** ***ELEANOR*** *exits.* ***JEKYLL*** *is now* ***LANYON,*** *and he freezes at the back of the stage as* ***UTTERSON*** *addresses the audience.*

UTTERSON *(To audience)* December 26th, 1895. Following Enfield's story of Hyde, I felt I should do some further investigation. My first port of call was Cavendish Square, that citadel of medicine, wherein Dr. Jekyll's colleague Hastings Lanyon made his home. Perhaps he might be able to shed some light on the name of Edward Hyde... I arrived promptly at eleven, and was greeted by the master of the house himself.

LANYON *moves to* ***UTTERSON.*** *We hear the faint sound of a piano and singing; Christmas Carols.*

LANYON My dear Gabriel! Compliments of the season old boy!

UTTERSON And to you.

LANYON I do hope this is a personal call. Drink?

***LANYON** turns and moves to the easy chair as **UTTERSON** addresses the audience.*

UTTERSON *(To audience)* After a little rambling talk and a bottle of good red wine, I led up to the subject that so preoccupied my mind…

LANYON Hyde, you say? No; never heard of him. Since my time, I'm afraid.

UTTERSON Shame. I was hoping that being Harry's oldest friend, you might –

LANYON Oldest friend? I suppose if you mean the person who made his acquaintance first, then yes, that would be me, but 'friend?'

UTTERSON You don't consider him so?

LANYON I consider him… a brilliant man, in many ways; he got me through medical school, there's no denying that, but…

A beat.

UTTERSON Go on…

LANYON Years ago, he and I… had a series of disagreements.

The piano and singing stops.

UTTERSON Professional?

LANYON Of course.

UTTERSON I thought you had a common interest?

LANYON Once, perhaps, but it is, oh, more than ten years since Henry Jekyll became too fanciful for me. Some of his ideas; his theories...

***ELEANOR** enters.*

Gabriel, I believe you've met my wife...?

A beat.

UTTERSON Once or twice, yes.

ELEANOR How do you do, Mr. Utterson?

UTTERSON Gabriel, please. And I'm well, thank you. Yourself?

LANYON She's much the same, aren't you?

ELEANOR *(Smiling)* Yes.

A beat.

UTTERSON *(To **ELEANOR**)* Was, er, was that you before?

ELEANOR I'm a little rusty.

LANYON Nonsense! She sounded beautiful. Wouldn't you agree?

ELEANOR Hastie, don't embarrass our guest...

UTTERSON Do you still perform?

ELEANOR I'm sorry?

UTTERSON On the wall... I saw playbills; I wondered... Eleanor O'Donnell, the Irish songbird... was that...? (you)

ELEANOR *(Smiling)* A different life.

UTTERSON Well... London's loss.

A beat.

LANYON We were just discussing Henry Jekyll. You remember him, don't you my dear?

ELEANOR Of course.

LANYON Tell me, does he have the cane I purchased for him when we both qualified? Black ash, with a silver falcon-head handle...

UTTERSON He uses it still.

LANYON *(Delighted)* Ah! More of a gentleman's cane than a walking aid of course, but he loved it nonetheless.

ELEANOR That's the first time you've mentioned his name without a sneer in years.

LANYON I don't suppose he was altogether mad at first.

ELEANOR Perhaps he was a man out of his time.

A slightly awkward pause. Tension.

If you will excuse me...

The men stand. ***ELEANOR*** *leaves the room.*

UTTERSON I think I'd better be getting back...

LANYON Do you think Henry Jekyll is out of his time? Or out of his mind?

UTTERSON We haven't spoken about medicine to any great degree.

LANYON A wise move. His kind of, of, of rubbish... he ought to have put all that behind him. You've had experience in that area, I recall.

UTTERSON My sister, yes. Before she died.

LANYON I am sorry to hear that. But you, my boy! So good to see you! Come on; I'll show you out...

LANYON *exits.* ***UTTERSON*** *turns to the audience.*

UTTERSON *(To audience)* I left Cavendish Square with a troubled mind. In the short time Hyde had known Dr. Jekyll, he had managed to garner enough trust to be granted the Doctor's entire fortune. Yet when I questioned Jekyll's staff, their knowledge of Hyde extended only to a couple of visits, and those very fleeting. No-one I spoke with knew or had heard of Edward Hyde to any great degree. I found myself wondering how, and at what point, this man appeared in Harry's life?

Music; lights. We are in Whitechapel. It's 1889. Outdoors; night. ***JEKYLL*** *enters at pace from the other side. He is wincing with pain, but trying not to show it. He has a newspaper under his arm. He stands and checks his pocket watch.* ***ELEANOR*** *is now* ***ANNIE****, a prostitute. She enters and spots* ***JEKYLL*** *alone...*

ANNIE Penny for your troubles, squire?

JEKYLL Ah; no. No.

ANNIE Penny for something else then.

JEKYLL You couldn't afford my troubles, madam.

ANNIE I was rather hoping you paid me.

She starts to move off, expecting him to follow.

JEKYLL I'm not... er...

ANNIE 'S all right; I ain't got no rampsman waiting.

JEKYLL Indeed; but that's not why I'm here.

ANNIE Might not be why you came, but I daresay I can change your mind.

She joins him downstage once more.

Come on; there's a tavern roundabouts... get me a glass of gin, warm me up, and I'll do the same for you, if you know what I mean.

JEKYLL My dear woman, as cold as it might be, I am not seeking pleasurable company.

ANNIE Well what you doing down here then? Square-rigged swell like you, you only comes down Whitechapel for one reason. And I know you ain't Saucy Jacky, cos no-one ever mentioned no stick.

JEKYLL Quite.

ANNIE I ain't no ladybird. I'm a proper woman, I am. I got kids to support. Have a heart, squire.

She puts her arm on his shoulder.

JEKYLL Unhand me, madam.

He fishes in his pocket and digs out a coin.

Here; here's sixpence. Now please, leave.

ANNIE *(Taking the coin)* What is it; don't you like me or something?

JEKYLL I'm sure you're lovely; I just…

***LANYON**, now once more played by **UTTERSON**, enters. His expression is grim.*

Hastie!

LANYON Expecting someone else?

***ANNIE** looks at the pair of them.*

ANNIE Oh, now I get it. Pity; you got pretty eyes.

*She sashays past **LANYON**, giving him the once-over.*

*(To **LANYON**)* You want to get back up West; there's clubs for your sort.

***ANNIE** exits.*

JEKYLL I assure you, Hastie, I am not in the habit of procuring the services of dollymops such as – (that woman there)

LANYON So this is where you meet, is it? Discuss your requirements.

JEKYLL I'm sorry?

LANYON You and Stevens. I know he lodges hereabouts…

JEKYLL I have no idea what you're – (talking about)

LANYON Don't.

A beat.

I saw you. The night before last.

JEKYLL Saw me…?

LANYON To be more specific, I followed you.

A beat.

JEKYLL	Where did you see me…?
LANYON	At the Endymion. With Stevens, and a boatman.

***JEKYLL** is stunned into silence.*

He's is supplying you with subjects, isn't he?

***JEKYLL** doesn't respond.*

How much are you paying him? Hmmm? Does he pick them for you, or do you simply take any you're offered?

*Still nothing from **JEKYLL**.*

Did you never think for one minute that it was time to give up?

JEKYLL	Give up?
LANYON	Three years you have been trying, Henry; three years. This, this business with astrocytes, it's a folly; a dead end!
JEKYLL	You're wrong.
LANYON	You put me in an impossible position.
JEKYLL	What would you do? Stop me?
LANYON	I would do more than that…

A beat.

Why, Henry? Why this?

JEKYLL I'm forty-one years old, and I move like a man twice my age. Look at me; my hands, they…

A beat.

I don't have a lot of time.

LANYON For what?

JEKYLL You know what I'm working on. You helped me; initially, at least.

LANYON Anything you did with the animals I supplied you with back at Bart's is on your conscience, not mine. I did not condone torture.

JEKYLL *(Scoffing)* Torture!

LANYON What would you call it?

JEKYLL Not quick enough.

LANYON What?

JEKYLL It wasn't quick enough; the work with animals. I have to move faster than that. I'm doing medicine people have never even dreamed of. If I'm right, this won't just change the face of our science; it will – (change the world)

LANYON Change the world? I've heard that before.

JEKYLL It's a whole new field; neurochemistry. Plain and simple.

LANYON You're killing people.

JEKYLL People die every day. Bloody Sunday; Jack the Ripper; the smallpox epidemic. Pick your tragedy.

He opens his newspaper.

Here; today's City Final.

LANYON What are you - ? (trying to prove)

JEKYLL "March 12th 1889. Carriage overturns in Rotherhithe; three fatalities." What do we do? What do you do? You move on, to the next patient... the next tragedy... try and win as many as you can. I am talking about an opportunity to alter life as we know it.

LANYON By killing people.

JEKYLL *(With a flash of anger)* Those people were already dead. I took them from a plague ship; gave them medicine, food, a warm bed – I brought them back to life. At that point, their lives, such as they were, became forfeit.

***LANYON** is speechless. A beat.*

If you could understand madness, in one or all of its forms, but you had to kill one person to make the breakthrough, wouldn't you have to? Hmmm? One life, and the mysteries of the brain are unravelled forever.

LANYON You don't get to decide who lives and dies. You are not God.

JEKYLL Envy does not become you, Dr. Lanyon.

LANYON This has nothing to do with envy!

JEKYLL Really?

LANYON Medicine is about preserving life.

JEKYLL What do you think it's all been about? Have you been aboard the Endymion, Hastie? Or the Atlas? Have you looked at the faces of those on either ship?

LANYON This isn't about those people...

JEKYLL Do you know anyone on board?

LANYON ... and it isn't about me.

JEKYLL One name. Give me one name.

A beat.

LANYON You know I can't.

JEKYLL I take people without families; mostly men; never children. I knew, and cared for, every one of the people I brought back to shore. Every one of the people I personally nursed back to health...

LANYON Before experimenting on them...

JEKYLL ...was a hero. They all – they all... were all – heroes.

LANYON They didn't choose to be.

JEKYLL Can we choose heroism? That's for future generations to decide. And when I'm finished, their names – all of them – will live forever.

LANYON Like yours?

A beat.

JEKYLL Hastie, if it were you...

LANYON If it were me, I would continue my research until I could find a route to my conclusions without torturing animals or killing people.

*Pause. **JEKYLL** knows the game is up.*

JEKYLL It's prison, then, is it?

LANYON Is that what you were expecting?

***JEKYLL** is silent.*

God knows it should be. What you have done stands against all I believe in, all the God-given principles of life, and mercy; but... I will spare you. You will not go to prison. Nor will any of this be mentioned ever again.

JEKYLL Thank you; thank you Hastie. I…

LANYON In return for my wife.

Silence. ***ELEANOR*** *enters in a spotlight, holding the mask. She softly sings the Irish folk ballad 'The Girl I left Behind Me.' It will underscore.*

ELEANOR *(Singing)* All the dames of France are fond and free
And Flemish lips are really willing
Very soft the maids of Italy
And Spanish eyes are so thrilling
Still, although I bask beneath their smile,
Their charms will fail to bind me
And my heart falls back to Erin's isle
To the girl I left behind me.

LANYON I may not be as brilliant as you, Henry, but I am not blind. I know what has developed between you. For two years I have been sharing a house, a bed – with a ghost; the spectre of my wife, created by my best friend. And as much as you love this twisted science of yours, that's nothing to the amount I love her. I love her, and I want her back.

A beat.

If you ever cared for me or for our friendship, then leave her alone; let her get the... poison of you out of her system. Do that and you will keep your freedom.

JEKYLL I'm not sure it's up to me...

LANYON Then make it up to you!

*Silently, **JEKYLL** nods his assent. **ELEANOR** stops singing.*

Tell her tomorrow.

JEKYLL Tomorrow?

LANYON She wouldn't miss your birthday.

ELEANOR Happy birthday. Here.

She holds out the mask. A beat.

LANYON Tell her.

***JEKYLL** nods again.*

ELEANOR What's wrong?

LANYON Then this is good-bye. I can't imagine we will be seeing much of each other beyond tonight.

***LANYON** offers his hand. **JEKYLL** takes it; numb. **LANYON** moves to exit.*

ELEANOR What's wrong, Henry?

JEKYLL *(Quietly)* I swear, once I complete my research, I –

***LANYON** turns.*

LANYON No. Henry; no. It's over.

ELEANOR What do you mean?

LANYON There will be no more research. Ever again. Not on a smallpox carrier, a dog, a rat…

ELEANOR But I thought this… I thought…

LANYON My poorer patients talk; loudly, often and without restraint. If I hear even the vaguest rumour of people going missing, or if I discover an unusual ordering pattern amongst the pharmacists and apothecaries of London, I will finish you. Is that clear enough?

***JEKYLL** nods.*

ELEANOR *(Crying)* Please, Henry… please…

JEKYLL I'm sorry.

The next two lines are almost spoken over one another.

LANYON Good-night, Dr. Jekyll.

ELEANOR Goodbye, Henry.

***ELEANOR** lays the mask on the chair nearest to her, and she and **LANYON** exit. Music. **JEKYLL** takes from the boxes another series of phials and bottles, addressing the audience as he mixes compounds together. By the time he has finished the speech, he is holding a flask of noxious looking liquid in his hands.*

JEKYLL *(To audience)* For six years I did nothing but theoretical research. Then, in April 1895, and following my parents' demise, I bought a house with some of the wealth I inherited. It had once belonged to a celebrated surgeon, and had separate out-buildings, so, unmolested, and in secret, I continued my work. I was consumed with it... but I needed a test subject... someone I could fully trust...

*There is the sound of a heartbeat. **JEKYLL** looks at the glass; wipes his mouth. He looks around nervously. Knows what he's got to do. Slowly he raises the beaker to his lips, but just as he is about to drink, there is a knocking (as if at the door), and the heartbeat sound stops abruptly.*

(Calling off) Yes?

BRADSHAW *(Off)* Begging your pardon, sir; there's been another delivery.

JEKYLL Come in.

BRADSHAW *enters with a small brown paper package.*

Set it down there, Miss Bradshaw.

BRADSHAW *does as she is told.*

BRADSHAW It's from Hook & Sons in Greenwich.

JEKYLL *(Preoccupied)* Is it?

BRADSHAW Oh, I wasn't prying, sir; it was only that my brother was apprenticed there, that's all. Only to fetch and carry, really; not to measure and whatnot. He isn't no pharmacist. Course, he'd like to be. He was saying to me on Tuesday, when – (I saw him last)

JEKYLL Miss Bradshaw?

BRADSHAW Sir?

JEKYLL That will be all.

BRADSHAW Oh. Oh; sorry, sir. Good afternoon.

BRADSHAW *curtseys and exits.* ***JEKYLL*** *makes a couple of recalculations in his head, jots something down on a piece of paper, takes a small measure from the equipment on the table, opens the parcel, takes a small amount from there and adds it to the glass.* ***UTTERSON*** *enters and watches from one upstage corner,* ***ELEANOR*** *from the other. The heartbeat begins once again.* ***JEKYLL*** *raises the glass to his lips, visibly trembling; and at the last minute…*

JEKYLL Damn it. Damn it!

...he slams it down on the table and exits. Music. Driving; insistent. Lights. ***UTTERSON*** *exits and* ***ELEANOR*** *moves downstage to address the audience.*

ELEANOR *(To audience)* 1895. Every year that had passed without Henry Jekyll the smile I wore grew more painful, as if the muscles that worked my cheeks were slowly squeezing my heart. It had become a pattern that I would look for reasons to escape the house at Cavendish Square; if only for a few hours. If ever there was a city on earth to feel alone with everyone, it is surely London. On June 26th, I happened to be at the Natural History Museum in South Kensington...

She starts to walk across the front of the stage as if looking at exhibits. ***JEKYLL*** *enters upstage.* ***ELEANOR*** *senses he is there. Stops. Does not turn round.*

(To ***JEKYLL****)* If you want to sneak up on someone unannounced, I suggest you wear a less distinctive cologne, Dr. Jekyll.

Pause.

JEKYLL Aren't you going to turn around?
ELEANOR Not yet.

Pause.

JEKYLL Shall I go…?

ELEANOR Not yet.

***JEKYLL** moves alongside. **ELEANOR** notices **JEKYLL** wincing with each step.*

How's your health?

JEKYLL I've been better.

ELEANOR You've not aged well.

JEKYLL Thank you.

ELEANOR I mean it; you look dire.

JEKYLL You look delightful.

*A beat. **ELEANOR** turns to face **JEKYLL**.*

I'm sorry; have I said the wrong thing?

ELEANOR You gave up on us for the good of the world. You cannot compliment me on my appearance and expect me to say, thank you kind sir, please forget the years you wasted.

JEKYLL I'm not expecting you to. Besides… my years have been wasted too.

A beat.

ELEANOR Meaning?
JEKYLL My research. I don't think I can carry on.

***ELEANOR** turns to face him.*

ELEANOR Why not?
JEKYLL I reached an impasse.
ELEANOR You're going to have to do better than that.
JEKYLL Very well, I lack the necessary resources.
ELEANOR I didn't mean your explanation.

Music, driving, soft at first but with growing intensity.

You can't give up.

JEKYLL I don't see that I have much choice.
ELEANOR Then you use what choices you do have, or you bend the rules.

*They look at one another for a second, then **ELEANOR** turns out front once again. **JEKYLL** leaves the scene and heads back up to his table, taking the cover from it. **UTTERSON** appears upstage and watches. He is in a spotlight. **JEKYLL** lifts and swirls the beaker, as **ELEANOR** continues to speak with **JEKYLL** as if he is still with her in the museum.*

I've had a long time to think about what I might say to you, and after six years I didn't think it was going to be this – you have to make your research count. That first night we met, when I took your side, it was because you made it personal for me.

***JEKYLL** wipes his lips, picks up the potion and downs it in one. A heartbeat is added to the mix.*

So maybe this isn't personal for me, and maybe I've lost everyone I ever cared about so there's no way it could be...

*Every word underlined in **JEKYLL's** next speech is spoken in a slurred voice by **UTTERSON** as well as **JEKYLL**.*

JEKYLL Increased blood-flow; adrenal gland in brain stimulated – head feeling heavy... head feeling heavy...

*Both **JEKYLL** and **UTTERSON** make a guttural, strangling noise at the same time. They are convulsing; twitching. The music now has a second heartbeat in it; this is the start of **HYDE**.*

ELEANOR ...but do you really want to go to your grave knowing you were this close to changing the world?

JEKYLL Solution breaking through blood-brain barrier... permeating cortex...

***JEKYLL** convulses. **UTTERSON** does the same.*

ELEANOR I read every paper you gave me, and your theories make sense.

JEKYLL Frontal lobe... uuurgh... temporal... temporal lobe... occipital... parietal... flooded with... flooded...

ELEANOR And if I had a relative with hysteria, or schizophrenia, or any other mania, I'd be pushing you now. I'd be pushing you hard.

***JEKYLL** and **UTTERSON** look up and out, as if seeing something dancing in their field of vision. They say the next lines not exactly in synch. They are maybe half a word to a word out.*

BOTH My God... it's full of stars...

***JEKYLL** and **UTTERSON** double over, groaning.*

ELEANOR I'd have understood the sacrifice you made then, and all your work and research... but I'll never understand you giving up.

BOTH Lights... too bright; mouth too dry. Taste of boiling rust...

*Slowly, they stand upright. **JEKYLL** looks at his own hand. With identical and flowing movement, **UTTERSON** looks at his hand.*

ELEANOR Can you think of nothing to say to me?

BOTH Is that my hand? It doesn't look like my hand...

ELEANOR Say something. Say something!

BOTH That's not my voice... is it?

ELEANOR Anything!

BOTH Muscles knitting; tightening... strength increasing...

They both make a grabbing movement with the same hand.

ELEANOR After everything we were to one another...

BOTH My... chest... I can... I can breathe!

They both take a deep, painless breath.

ELEANOR Goodbye Dr. Jekyll.

***ELEANOR** exits. Both **JEKYLL** and **UTTERSON** stand up straight and laugh. **UTTERSON** eventually stops laughing as **JEKYLL**'s laughter has changed. The music ends, and **JEKYLL** allows the cane to go crashing to the floor. He moves around the space, touching things before reaching into one of the crates for a hand mirror.*

HYDE *(Looking at himself)* Who are you?

He touches his face, looking at himself from every angle, then snatches up the mask and exits. Music – loud and dramatic.

UTTERSON *exits as* ***ELEANOR*** *enters and addresses the audience.*

ELEANOR *(To audience)* After my encounter, I felt more adrift than ever. I decided to revisit my old haunt; Wilton's Music Hall. Upon leaving by the side entrance, I found myself staring into the face of the devil...

HYDE *enters, now wearing the devil mask.* ***ELEANOR*** *walks through the chairs as if exiting the theatre.* ***HYDE*** *comes around the side of them.* ***ELEANOR*** *catches sight of the figure in the mask.*

(To ***HYDE****)* Not very gentlemanly to sneak up on someone. Especially not twice in one day.

HYDE *doesn't move. Stares only.*

I'm assuming you followed me for a reason. I hope it's an apology.

Still nothing from ***HYDE.*** ***ELEANOR*** *is now slightly unsettled. She refers to the mask.*

I can't believe you still have that.

He remains mute; impassive.

Henry?

HYDE *(Laughing)* My name is Edward Hyde.
ELEANOR What have you done with Henry?

***HYDE** takes the mask off. **ELEANOR** looks him in the eyes.*

Jesus Mary mother of God!

*She moves away. **HYDE** approaches her. He smiles and looks her up and down. A beat. She turns.*

How did you do it?

He does not reply. Moves closer.

This is beyond... you must be...

*With one quick movement **HYDE** grabs her and kisses her. She breaks away.*

No; you don't just...

HYDE I am so... hungry.

He kisses her again. This time she gives in a little, then breaks off.

Coward.

ELEANOR What?

HYDE You heard.

He backs away from her, still meeting her gaze.

If you want me, come and find me...

He pulls on the Devil mask and exits the way he came, laughing.

ELEANOR *(To audience)* And he was gone, into the night, all aggression and arrogance, swinging Henry's cane like a cudgel. Before it had been so abruptly curtailed, our... love... had been no less passionate, no less true for not being physically consummated. This, though... this was something else. And though my immediate reaction was one of revulsion, I have to admit... when I knew it was Henry, a part of me leapt inside...

Music. ***ELEANOR*** *exits.* ***UTTERSON*** *enters, moves the chairs back together and adds the third to create the park bench. He sits.*

UTTERSON *(To audience)* February 1896. From Boxing Day onwards my dreams had been tormented. So I resolved to haunt the door in the by-street. Meet the fellow myself.

Business was slow, affording me the opportunity to linger both day and night. If he be Mr. Hyde, I thought, I shall be Mr. Seek.

A beat.

At ten o'clock on the fifth night, my patience was rewarded. It was a fine, dry evening, frost in the air; and I had scarce been on the bench a few minutes when I was aware of an odd light footstep drawing near.

The sound of footsteps is head, echoing on cobbles.

I watched, my heart pounding. The steps drew closer, and I saw what manner of man I had to deal with. He made straight for the door, drawing a key as he went. This was my man.

***JEKYLL** enters as **HYDE**. **UTTERSON** stands.*

*(To **HYDE**)* Mr. Hyde, I think.

*A beat. **HYDE** stands to his full height, but does not turn.*

HYDE That's my name. What do you want?

UTTERSON I… am an old companion of Dr. Jekyll's – Mr. Utterson, of Gaunt Street.

HYDE If you're on your way to see him, don't bother. He's out.

UTTERSON It wasn't the good doctor I came to see. I thought – if he'd mentioned me – that you might consider admitting me.

HYDE How did you know me?

UTTERSON We have common friends.

HYDE Who?

UTTERSON Well; Jekyll, for one…

HYDE Told you what I look like, did he? Where to find me?

UTTERSON Yes…

***HYDE** turns and faces **UTTERSON**, staring at him fixedly.*

HYDE You're a liar!

UTTERSON Come, sir; that is not fitting language.

***HYDE** stares at **UTTERSON** for a moment, then laughs. **UTTERSON** forces a smile.*

Well! Now I shall know you again.

HYDE Will you?

UTTERSON Yes.

HYDE Here.

***HYDE** holds a card out for **UTTERSON**.*

My address. It's as well we've met.

UTTERSON Indeed.

***HYDE** drops the card on the floor and exits.* ***UTTERSON** picks it up and turns to the audience.*

(To audience) With extraordinary quickness, he had unlocked the door and disappeared inside.

***UTTERSON** sits.*

The moment I left his company I found myself slick with sweat, and filled with murderous desire. I walked through London's quiet streets, rounding corner after corner, turning it over in my mind; his manner... his displeasing smile, the tone of his voice. He was glad I had his address? Why would he want a lawyer he had never met to have his address? He had to have been thinking of the Will. That must be why, as well as the location on the card, he had secured a bolt-hole so close to Harry's... house...

***UTTERSON's** expression changes. Something has just occurred to him. Music.*

My God; how had I not seen it sooner? The little-used door was just around the corner from Jekyll's house... Jekyll's house with the out-buildings... and Hyde had a key!

UTTERSON *reconfigures the stage as he talks.*

I dashed across the courtyard, past the outbuildings to the main body of the house and rang the doorbell. As ever, Harry's manservant, Poole, answered the door...

JEKYLL *enters as* ***POOLE****, an older man; loyal and dependable.*

POOLE Good evening, sir.

UTTERSON Is Dr. Jekyll at home, Poole?

POOLE I will see. Will you wait here by the fire, sir? Or shall I give you a light in the dining room?

UTTERSON Here, thank you.

POOLE *exits.*

(To audience) I stood a moment by the fire in the hall, the face of Hyde hanging heavy on my memory. Even the flickering firelight seemed to exude an air of menace. I was lost, and tired, and confused.

***POOLE** returns.*

POOLE	I'm afraid Dr. Jekyll is out, sir.
UTTERSON	But... I saw Mr. Hyde go in. Is that right? When Dr. Jekyll is from home, I mean.
POOLE	Quite right, sir. He has a laboratory key. We see very little of him on this side of the house.
UTTERSON	Your master seems to place a great deal of trust in this fellow, Poole.
POOLE	He does indeed, sir. We all have orders to obey him.
UTTERSON	Right... well, good-night, Poole.
POOLE	Good-night, sir.

***POOLE** exits. **UTTERSON** turns back to the audience.*

UTTERSON	*(To audience)* I had to talk to Jekyll again. The following day I called to see him. And the day after, and the day after that... there was no sign of him.

*We hear a woman giggling. **UTTERSON** reconfigures the stage.*

Two weeks he was away from home. I had seen the loathsome Hyde cross the courtyard once as I was leaving, but was pleased to have avoided him.

***HYDE** enters, shirt open at the collar, swigging a bottle of whisky.*

HYDE *(Calling off)* Get in here!

The girl giggles again.

UTTERSON *(To audience)* I asked around some of the less reputable establishments in the area surrounding Hyde's place of residence. They had all seen him there; not one of them had a good word to say for him. He had been busy; visiting gin parlours, gambling dens…

HYDE *(Calling off)* I said get in!

UTTERSON *(To audience)* …and brothels…

*The owner of the giggle is **ANNIE**. She enters coyly.*

ANNIE Sorry, squire; I was just finishing my mother's ruin…

***HYDE** walks towards her with a twisted grin on his face.*

'Ere, are you all right? You look awful queer.

HYDE All right? I'm… capital!

He swigs from the bottle. He's very close now.

ANNIE You're not going to hurt me or nothing, are you?

HYDE Oh, I would imagine so.

ANNIE What?

***HYDE** laughs.*

Only... only I'm expected. I think – I think I'd better be going...

*She turns to leave. **HYDE** catches her arm.*

Help!

HYDE No-one's going to hear you. My housekeeper's a trifle deaf, you see...

He pushes her to the ground. She starts to crawl towards the exit.

ANNIE No... no... you can't... I have kids...

HYDE There is no can't.

She exits.

You will find the door locked, I'm afraid...

***HYDE** moves upstage and freezes, arm raised. Offstage, **ANNIE** screams. We hear a soundscape of music, echo, screams and violence, at the end of which, **HYDE** says:*

Here. Here's your bloody sixpence.

He exits. Music calms.

UTTERSON *(To audience)* A fortnight after my initial approach to the house, in late February 1896, I finally found my friend at home. It was clear as soon as I set eyes upon him, however, that the doctor did not share any of my concerns regarding Edward Hyde. On the contrary, Harry Jekyll looked as if he didn't have a care in the world...

***JEKYLL** enters, smiling. **UTTERSON** exits. As he goes, the smile on **JEKYLL**'s face drops. He turns to the audience.*

JEKYLL *(To audience)* Hyde was more than I could have hoped for; not only an incredible resource for examining astrocyte activity... but also an outlet for my darker dreams and desires. I knew that the scientific world would not recognise the benefits of something so... unstable, so, for now, I kept my research to myself. I was working on stabilising agents for the second testing phase, but the first batch of the formula... the pure batch... I kept. I had to. I felt younger, happier; lighter in body... to go from this shell, with all its imperfections and flaws, to physical release... was intoxicating.

***JEKYLL** reconfigures the stage.*

As time wore on, though, Hyde's violence washed over my daily existence like a crippling fever; holding me in its thrall. The research was one thing, but what I was seeing through Hyde's eyes made the pure science increasingly hard to justify.

A beat.

It was for this reason I stopped the transformations, and for the next three months I was solely Jekyll, compiling from memory any and all data I could about the effects on the brain... then, one wet Tuesday afternoon in September 1896 I arrived at the house I had bought as Hyde. My intention was to dismiss the housekeeper and sell the place, when I was surprised by a visitor. With two words I was undone...

***ELEANOR** enters. Fixes him with a seductive stare.*

ELEANOR Show me.
JEKYLL Eleanor...

ELEANOR Show me.

JEKYLL You don't know what you're asking me...

ELEANOR Yes I do.

JEKYLL No; I made this happen for the wrong reasons.

ELEANOR Show me.

JEKYLL Listen; when I took the formula, I was hoping to discover the secrets of the mind. All I have learned is that the good half of me slumbered whilst the darker half, kept awake by ambition, took its chance.

ELEANOR Meaning you're all good...?

She puts her arms around him. He is fighting with his conscience. Music plays.

JEKYLL No! That's just it! I'm still me; I'm not purely good... but Edward Hyde? He is as close to true evil as you're ever likely to come.

ELEANOR I want to see it.

JEKYLL I can't control it.

ELEANOR I don't want you to control it.

JEKYLL Please...

ELEANOR Show me. You want to. I know you do. I want you to.

JEKYLL Don't make me...

***ELEANOR** has reached into his pocket and pulled out a silver hip-flask.*

ELEANOR Do it. Or I will.

She starts to take the lid from the flask.

You said you wanted human subjects.

JEKYLL You don't understand it.

ELEANOR I'll tell you what I do understand. I understand that every time Hastie touches me, every tiny compliment paid, or hint of discord shown… I'm… and then you come back into my life, show me this jewel… and disappear!

JEKYLL I'm sorry… just… don't…

ELEANOR I'm not afraid any more. I don't care. And if it takes being someone else, so be it. Most days I can think of nothing better.

*She raises the flask to her lips, but **JEKYLL** takes it from her.*

JEKYLL No! Give it to me!

***ELEANOR** hands him the flask and he drinks it at once. He shivers again, stands upright. The cane falls to the floor once again. He draws **ELEANOR** to him and kisses her roughly.*

*(As **HYDE**)* I'll destroy you.

ELEANOR You destroyed me years ago.

HYDE Not like this…

He kisses her again.

Wait there.

ELEANOR What are you –
HYDE Wait!

***HYDE** exits. **ELEANOR** turns to the audience. Music.*

ELEANOR *(To audience)* I had dreamt of nothing else in months... sick with the thought that this thing existed, but fascinated, aroused by it. As dangerous as Edward Hyde was, at least there was connection, and that's what I needed. So it was that my affair with this physical beast began. It was perfect. I was happy again, after a fashion. And on the extremely rare occasion that our paths crossed socially, I would exchange cordialities with Dr. Jekyll, and leave Hastie none the wiser...

***JEKYLL** enters. **ELEANOR** passes him as she heads offstage.*

Doctor.

JEKYLL *(Nodding)* Mrs. Lanyon.

***ELEANOR** exits. **JEKYLL** sits, head in hands. Looks at the audience.*

(To audience) I knew the duplicity would come at a price, but I did not expect it to be so great. One night in late November 1896, I bid Poole, Miss Bradshaw and the others goodnight and retired to my bed as usual... only to awake the next morning knowing something was wrong. My joints felt loose; strong; my hands gnarled and tough. Without the solution passing my lips, I was Hyde!

He stands and immediately starts the change, fighting it as he narrates.

It seemed... seemed that... where once I needed... the... drug to become Hyde, now I needed it to remain Henry Jekyll. It was time to realise... to recognise... that perhaps I was never the rational scientist; never Dr. Jekyll...

He doubles over, stands up again.

I was always the beast, who once dreamt I was... a man...

Suddenly the fight is over, and it is ***HYDE*** *who is talking to us.*

(As ***HYDE****; to audience)* And now the dream is over. For how do you tell a butterfly he must return to the chrysalis? Do you imagine he'd go quietly?

Music swells. ***UTTERSON*** *enters as* ***CAREW****, an elderly politician, with a shuffling gait and a soft and pleasant voice. He wears a top hat, which he tips to* ***HYDE****. He is upstage,* ***HYDE*** *downstage, facing out.*

CAREW Good evening, my fine fellow…

HYDE *doesn't respond.*

Another night-owl, I see? I must admit to being fond of the night air myself…

CAREW *joins* ***HYDE*** *centre-stage. Music plays.* ***ELEANOR*** *appears upstage, singing an Irish ballad.*

HYDE What's that?
CAREW The night air; rather bracing.

CAREW *looks at the cane* ***HYDE*** *is swinging in his hands.*

That's a fine looking cane, sir.

HYDE Is it? Sir.

CAREW I meant no offence.

***HYDE** laughs darkly.*

Perhaps I'll be off. I'll bid you goodnight.

HYDE No, Sir. Allow me to bid it to you...

*A stylised piece of physical theatre, music building, **ELEANOR** singing, perhaps the same refrain on a loop as, with choreographed precision, **HYDE** hits **CAREW**, knocking him to the ground, then beating, punching and stamping on him... the last thing the audience see before the interval is **HYDE**, bestriding **CAREW**'s stricken body, breaking his cane in two. Lights fade to black, the music plays, still building as the cast clear, then the music stops abruptly and the house lights and pre-set are snapped up.*

End of Act One.

*Act Two. The stage has been reconfigured; we are in **HYDE's** chambers in Soho. Music plays; driving, insistent; picking up tonally where we left Act One. Lights fade to black and **ELEANOR** enters, holding the mask in her hands and pacing. As the music subsides, we hear a clock chime three. **ELEANOR** sits; stands. **HYDE** enters, his jacket removed, his shirt slick with blood. Blood is also around his mouth, all over his hands and he clutches one half of the cane we saw him break at the end of the previous act. Music fades as **ELEANOR** sees him. She gives out a shriek.*

HYDE Why are you still here?

ELEANOR What happened? Are you hurt?

***HYDE** dumps the half a cane in the nearest crate and starts to remove his shirt.*

Henry?

HYDE *(Bellowing)* Don't use that name!

ELEANOR Sorry.

HYDE And don't apologise. It's weak. Watch the windows!

***ELEANOR** moves downstage as if watching the window. **HYDE** takes his shirt off, wipes his face and hands with it.*

What are you waiting around for? We both got what we wanted.

ELEANOR Whose blood is that?

HYDE Not mine.

ELEANOR What have you done?

HYDE Indulged.

*He throws the shirt at **ELEANOR**, goes to a crate, removes one and starts to put it on.*

Get rid of that.

ELEANOR How?

HYDE I don't care. Burn it. Burn everything.

ELEANOR Here?

***HYDE** does not reply.*

Did you kill someone?

A pause.

HYDE Yes.

ELEANOR In a fight?

HYDE Why do you care?

ELEANOR Because if you were attacked, and retaliated –

HYDE I wasn't attacked. I attacked. I battered and kicked and gouged and crushed and I enjoyed it.

ELEANOR My God, who was it?

HYDE I don't know. I only know he's dead, and I don't want to be.

***ELEANOR** drops the shirt.*

I need to return to the cripple again. Understand?

***ELEANOR** nods.*

Good. And since you're still here, I assume you're willing to aid in my disappearance. Burn the shirt, burn the chequebooks; anything that can connect me to him... and go.

***ELEANOR** moves towards him.*

ELEANOR When will I see you?
HYDE Keep watch, damn you!

***ELEANOR** moves back to her downstage position*

See me? There is no 'see me' ever again. This is the end of Edward Hyde; understand? If I am found, I am for the gallows.

ELEANOR But what about...?
HYDE The cripple won't see you. He can't. Go back to Lanyon. Throw yourself on his mercy. He's got no pride; he'll accept you.
ELEANOR I can't. It's too far gone...
HYDE Not my concern.

ELEANOR Perhaps we could emigrate… you could come with me to Ireland, or…

HYDE Listen! Understand! I am going to disappear. And you are going to forget about me. I will not die; not for this, not for you, not for anything.

He touches his head, closes one eye. Danse Macabre plays faintly.

I can feel him, in here, crying… it's pathetic. Like a child in a locked room.

ELEANOR Edward…

HYDE Watch the window!

He roughly tucks his shirt into his trousers.

I'm going. Wait half an hour before you leave.

She looks back at him. Danse Macabre fades.

Look on me for the last time. You will never see me again.

He bows low and exits. ***ELEANOR*** *throws the shirt into one of the crates, sits and buries her face in her hands, shaking with sobs. There is the sound of knocking. Music. The sound of police whistles. Recording of newspaper vendors crying "Murder! Murder in Eastcheap! Read all about it! Violent* *bloody murder!" **ELEANOR** wipes her face and exits as **UTTERSON** enters and reconfigures the space. He sets two of the chairs face-to-face downstage, returns centre and addresses the audience.*

UTTERSON *(To audience)* For months, nothing was seen or heard of the odious phantom. We all held our breath that he may have gone forever... then, early one Saturday morning in February 1897, I was awoken at my house on Gaunt Street by a sharp, insistent pummelling on the door.

*Another knock. **JEKYLL** enters. He is now Inspector **NEWCOMEN** of Scotland Yard.*

NEWCOMEN You are a Mr. Gabriel Utterson, of 24 Gaunt Street?

UTTERSON I am.

NEWCOMEN My name is Inspector Newcomen of Scotland Yard. Forgive the intrusion.

UTTERSON Of course.

***NEWCOMEN** steps towards **UTTERSON**.*

Could I get you anything? Perhaps a drink, or...?

NEWCOMEN Mr. Utterson, I am here on the gravest of business. There has been... a crime... hereabouts, and... inasmuch as, well, the victim is known, at least to some, in his professional capacity, I'm afraid he may be known to you personally. And yes, actually, could I trouble you for a tot of rum, sir?

__UTTERSON__ takes a glass and bottle from one of the crates and pours whilst talking.

UTTERSON Am I to understand there has been a murder?

NEWCOMEN I'm afraid that's putting it rather mildly, sir. This... this looks more like some kind of annihilation.

With trembling hand, __NEWCOMEN__ takes the glass, and downs it in one shot.

Thank you.

UTTERSON More?

NEWCOMEN No. Yes.

He gives the glass back to __UTTERSON__.

To return to why I'm here, the victim had in his possession a sealed and stamped envelope with your name and address on it.

UTTERSON My God; who is it?

NEWCOMEN We believe... it is the MP, Sir Denvers Carew.

NEWCOMEN *takes the refilled glass and drinks.*

UTTERSON Sir Denvers is indeed a client, yes. He was due to meet me in a week or so, on a matter of conveyancing.

NEWCOMEN *takes the bottle from* ***UTTERSON*** *and refills his glass whilst talking.*

NEWCOMEN I wonder if you might accompany me to the police station, sir. We are hoping you might assist a formal identification.

UTTERSON *addresses the audience as the pair of them move down to the chairs.*

UTTERSON *(To audience)* It didn't take us long to reach the place where the body had been carried.

NEWCOMEN *mimes holding a cloth back for* ***UTTERSON*** *to see. Clearly the sight is truly hideous. His words catch in his throat.*

(To ***NEWCOMEN****)* Yes, I recognise him. I am sorry to say that this is Sir Denvers

Carew. What… what sort of a beast would do this to another human being?

NEWCOMEN Honestly, we don't know. See how the lower jaw is almost completely torn from the victim's face? That would take considerable strength and fury, that would. The extensive bruising on the body looks to be on account of his being trampled, and – and the bite-marks in one cheek…

UTTERSON Yes, yes, I understand.

*With some relief, **NEWCOMEN** puts the sheet back.*

What now? Are there witnesses; do you have anything in your favour…?

NEWCOMEN One; a young chambermaid at a property near the scene of the crime – she saw the whole thing from her window. And the only clue we have…

***NEWCOMEN** takes from one of the crates the other half of the walking cane, snapped in the middle, the falcon-head top matted with blood.*

…is this; left at the scene.

UTTERSON May I…?

He takes the cane. Looks at it gravely.

The witness – did she describe the assailant?

NEWCOMEN More than that, she named him. Said he had had occasion to call upon her master in the past. Have you heard the name Edward Hyde at all?

A beat.

UTTERSON Inspector Newcomen, I think I can take you to his house.

NEWCOMEN Lead on…

They turn the chairs around, climb upon them and sit on the backs. ***NEWCOMEN*** *mimes taking the reins.* ***UTTERSON*** *turns to the audience.*

UTTERSON *(To audience)* It was about nine in the morning. The first fog of the season; haggard shafts of daylight cutting through the pall, like a district of some city in a nightmare. The terror in my eyes was matched by that of Newcomen as we rounded the corner of the Soho street given as the address on Hyde's card. The fog lifted a little, showing a gin palace, a low French eating house, and ragged children of many nationalities huddled in doorways.

NEWCOMEN *pulls at the reins.* ***UTTERSON*** *moves the chairs.*

We climbed from the cab and approached the door.

NEWCOMEN *knocks on a crate upstage.*

NEWCOMEN Open up in there!

UTTERSON *(To audience)* This was the house of Harry's favourite, I thought. Heir to a quarter of a million sterling, and property besides.

NEWCOMEN *(To audience)* Open up in the name of the law!

ELEANOR *enters as* ***ANNIE****. She now sports an eye-patch.*

ANNIE You don't want to go in there, squire. Stay away.

UTTERSON Do you know the gentleman that lives here?

ANNIE He ain't no gentleman. He's a demon. Left me for dead, he did. Dragged me in an alley and left me.

NEWCOMEN You can consider yourself lucky.

ANNIE Lucky? Lucky? He took my eye!

NEWCOMEN Madam, we are investigating murder.

ANNIE Oh, don't worry – I didn't think you was down here on my account. We're just making up the numbers, we are.

She adjusts her shawl.

Now if you'll excuse me, I'm on my way for a morning glass...

***ANNIE** exits.*

NEWCOMEN Come then, Mr. Utterson, sir – let's be about it!

***NEWCOMEN** moves upstage.*

UTTERSON *(To audience)* The housekeeper, a grim-faced woman, showed us into Hyde's residence; two well-furnished rooms which bore every mark of having been recently ransacked: clothes lay about the floor, their pockets inside-out, lock-fast drawers stood open, and on the hearth there lay a pile of grey ashes, as though many papers had been burned... the charred remnants of the blaze including the stub-end of a cheque book.

NEWCOMEN Look at this!

***UTTERSON** turns. **NEWCOMEN** has taken the other half of the cane that **HYDE** dumped in the crate out, and holds it in his hand.*

It appears we have our man.

UTTERSON Most definitely.

NEWCOMEN He must have lost his head, or he never would have left the stick, or, above all, burned the cheque book. Money's life to a man on the run. I have him in my hand, sir. We have nothing to do but wait for him at the bank.

***NEWCOMEN** shakes **UTTERSON**'s hand.*

Sir, you have been a great help. *(Quieter)* And, ah, thanks for the rum...

***NEWCOMEN** exits.*

UTTERSON *(To audience)* Terrified for my friend, I accepted a lift to Jekyll's place of residence. Poole admitted me, and led me down by the kitchen offices and across a yard to the medical outbuildings. It was my first visit to this part of my friend's quarters, and I was astonished. The walls were covered in crudely scrawled formulae, the floor littered with crates and strewn with packing straw. At the far end, a flight of stairs led to a door covered with red baize. Within, next to a blazing fire, was Dr. Jekyll…

***JEKYLL** enters, moving dreadfully. He sits with some difficulty.*

Even before he saw me, as he shuffled from a chalk-board back to his chair, I realised he was ill. Such deterioration – he looked deathly sick! He did not rise to meet me once settled, but held out a cold hand to beckon me closer…

JEKYLL Come… come in, come in. Pull up a chair, if you can find one…

***UTTERSON** moves a chair near to where **JEKYLL** sits.*

I was working, and… I have… some excellent results from a formula test…

UTTERSON Harry; you're in no fit state!

A beat.

You've heard the news?

JEKYLL Just now. They were crying in the square.

UTTERSON One word; Carew was my client, but so are you, and I want to know what I'm doing.

Tell me you haven't been mad enough to hide this fellow.

JEKYLL John, I swear to God... I swear to God I will never set eyes on him again.

UTTERSON Do you have any idea where he might be?

JEKYLL Safe. Quite safe.

UTTERSON Safe? Are you aware... do you have any clue...? If you had seen what I saw; what he had done to poor Danvers...

JEKYLL You do not know him as I do.

UTTERSON I pray I never shall.

JEKYLL All you need to know is that it is at an end. He does not want my help and will never more be heard of.

UTTERSON For your sake I hope you're right.

JEKYLL I... I am. I have grounds for certainty that I cannot... share with anyone. But there is one... one thing on which you may advise me.

UTTERSON Go on.

JEKYLL I have received a letter... and am at a loss whether to show it to the police.

UTTERSON A letter... from Hyde?

JEKYLL nods.

When did you get it...?

JEKYLL This morning, I believe.

UTTERSON	And you're afraid the letter will lead to his detection?
JEKYLL	I don't care what happens to him anymore; I'm done with him. I was thinking of my own character, which this hateful business has rather exposed…
UTTERSON	Let me see it.

***JEKYLL** reaches into his pocket for the letter…*

JEKYLL	I'm afraid I burned the envelope before I thought what I was about. But it bore no postmark. It was hand delivered.

*…and hands it to **UTTERSON**, who reads it silently.*

	I wish you to judge for me entirely whether to hand the letter to the police. I have… lost confidence in myself…

***UTTERSON** looks up from the letter.*

UTTERSON	This "means of escape" he mentions… that has nothing to do with you?
JEKYLL	Nothing at all.

***UTTERSON** returns to reading again temporarily, then finishes and looks back at **JEKYLL**.*

UTTERSON	I shall sleep on this.

JEKYLL Of course; your choice.

***UTTERSON** stands.*

UTTERSON One last thing. It was Hyde who dictated the terms in your will about the disappearance; correct?

***JEKYLL** nods. Sways; he is faint.*

I knew it. He meant to murder you. You had a fine escape.

JEKYLL More than that, I have had a lesson. Oh God, what a lesson I have had!

***JEKYLL** buries his face in his hands.*

UTTERSON *(To audience)* I left Jekyll by the fire, shivering and sobbing. On my way out I asked Poole if he had seen who had delivered the note… he wasn't aware of any such delivery. A sinking feeling grew in my gut. The hand that scribed the note was not dissimilar to the good doctor's own. Harry Jekyll forge for a murderer? He couldn't… could he…?

*Music. **UTTERSON** exits. **JEKYLL** looks up. His tears turn to laughter, and he stands. He is **HYDE**.*

HYDE *(To audience)* March, 1897. With supplies of the formula running low, I had to ensure I used what I had left properly. It didn't seem to matter about the size or frequency of the doses taken, the invalid hiding place was not sustaining, and I was reappearing at will; where once I'd convulse, the journey now was barely a shrug; a momentary loss of focus and I was out; unmasked. I'd always been there. He'd just given me a name.

He moves chairs, creating a different space, then swirls a hip-flask whilst addressing the audience.

Sometimes I'd be gone for days at a time; others, mere hours. And that would never do. So…

He drinks the formula, winces, then leans more heavily on the cane he was previously only carrying as an affectation.

*(As **JEKYLL**)* …in the time I had left as Henry Jekyll, I intended to do some good; redress the balance… I began giving time and money to charities and benevolent funds, I attended church; I made an anonymous donation to Carew's family… and on March 28th I threw a party, as a way of repairing old friendships…

Lights. ***LANYON*** *and* ***ELEANOR*** *enter holding champagne flutes.*

LANYON Henry.
JEKYLL Thank you for coming.
LANYON Of course.

They are awkward around each other.

How have you been?

JEKYLL Never better.

JEKYLL *approaches* ***LANYON****; shakes his hand.*

It's been too long.

LANYON Indeed.
JEKYLL And you; are you well? How is your practice?
LANYON I muddle through, as always. And Eleanor is well, aren't you, my dear?

ELEANOR *smiles compliantly; she is clearly bursting to say something.*

Still tolerating my favours, at least.

JEKYLL I'm sure it's more than that.
LANYON Perhaps you might give us a song later…

JEKYLL It's not necessary; you're both here to relax. See, most of our former colleagues are here; our contemporaries.

LANYON Yes, I was just speaking with Stevens – he was at Salpetriere a few years ago, working with Charcot before his passing.

JEKYLL *(Self-deprecating)* Ah! The French Jekyll.

LANYON *(Smiling at the memory)* Yes.

A beat. They clearly both want to say something to each other.

Henry –

JEKYLL Please… don't.

LANYON Perhaps if I'd have been a little more supportive…

JEKYLL Or perhaps if I had.

LANYON I know how much it would have meant to you, old boy.

***LANYON** and **JEKYLL** smile at one another.*

It is good to see you.

JEKYLL I cannot begin to express it. I confess when I dispatched the invitation, I hardly expected you to attend.

LANYON You have Utterson to thank for that.

JEKYLL Really?

LANYON He called upon me, told me what a changed man you are...

ELEANOR Quite changed.

A beat.

JEKYLL He's here tonight; I shall thank him in person.

LANYON You won't have long; I believe he said he was leaving before nine.

JEKYLL Then I shall do it now.

LANYON Follow me; he was last seen in the dining room...

They have exited. ***ELEANOR*** *turns to the audience.*

ELEANOR *(To audience)* All night I was avoided. He could barely bring himself to look at me. I watched him talk and laugh with other guests at his party, and felt I might throw up. He was mine and I his; heart... soul... and secrets...

JEKYLL *enters alone, laughing as if falling from one conversation in another room to this one.* ***ELEANOR*** *turns to him. They look at one another.*

JEKYLL I did not expect to see you.

ELEANOR The invitation was for both of us...

JEKYLL I thought you might have made some excuse.

ELEANOR Excuse?

Pause.

There was a reward offered.

JEKYLL I saw.

ELEANOR One thousand pounds. "For information leading to the apprehension of Edward Hyde."

JEKYLL Please... don't mention his name.

A beat.

ELEANOR The stories... in the press, about some of your – his, exploits...

He nods.

All of them?

He nods.

My God.

JEKYLL Well, he's gone now, so...

ELEANOR For good?

JEKYLL Yes. Yes. For good.

ELEANOR And you didn't think about contacting me?

A beat.

It's been over a month...

***JEKYLL** is uncomfortable.*

JEKYLL I should... attend... the other guests...

ELEANOR Oh, please – we are past that old difficulty, aren't we?

JEKYLL I have no desire to cause upset.

ELEANOR It's too late for that.

***JEKYLL** rounds on her.*

JEKYLL What do you want, Eleanor?

A beat.

You drew me back into a world I had abandoned.

ELEANOR Don't do that. Don't you dare. I found you at his house. I found you there.

JEKYLL I had gone there to close up, and instead...

ELEANOR What? You opened up?

A beat.

You had a choice. Just like the first time. Then and now, you had a choice.

JEKYLL He started this; not me.

ELEANOR He is you!

A beat.

Six years, I hadn't seen you; six years... and you...

JEKYLL I meant only to speak with you. Hyde; I have no control over...

ELEANOR How convenient.

JEKYLL You... drew him out of me...

ELEANOR You wanted to show me.

JEKYLL And look where it led.

A beat.

I am suffering just as much as you; believe me.

ELEANOR You look fine.

JEKYLL Because I smile in front of guests? In front of... (Hastie)

ELEANOR Then tell me what you feel!

JEKYLL No.

ELEANOR Tell me!

JEKYLL No.

ELEANOR Come on!

JEKYLL What do you want to hear? That I wish I had been less driven; that I had looked on at your wedding in envy, imagined us together? That I still do?

ELEANOR Do you?

JEKYLL Sometimes. All right? Sometimes. But sometimes isn't good enough for either of us.

Pause.

ELEANOR So that's it, then?

A beat.

JEKYLL It was never my intention... to... I didn't expect you to come...

ELEANOR Remind you, do I? Of Carew?

JEKYLL That was not me. I was not in control.

ELEANOR You keep telling yourself that.

JEKYLL You cannot possibly know what it is to be Hyde.

ELEANOR I know he's not a coward.

JEKYLL You're wrong. Edward Hyde is more cowardly than anyone you could meet. But I'm happy to say you will not meet him again.

A beat.

If you will excuse me.

***JEKYLL** exits. Music. **ELEANOR** turns to the audience.*

ELEANOR *(To audience)* I wanted to run through his house screaming at the top of my voice, exposing all his secrets, laying him bare before his peers. I wanted to beat him; tear him apart. I wanted to hurt him. But not as much as I wanted to consume him. Even after everything I'd been through, the idea of a life without him was more dreadful than one with him in it.

A beat. She sits.

There followed a month of dark moods and reflection; sickness and revelation. Then a letter came from Ireland; my mother, with whom I'd become estranged, was on her death-bed and asking for me. If I had been looking to make a change, there would be no better time…

LANYON *enters. Sits and opens a newspaper. Lights.*

LANYON I do wish you would let me examine you, dear.

ELEANOR I'm fine.

LANYON The idea that you would travel in this nervous state…

ELEANOR It's not really my choice.

LANYON You're sure you don't want me to accompany you?

ELEANOR You have your patients, and...

Pause.

...and I may stay on in Ireland for a while.

LANYON Take as much time as you need.
ELEANOR But what if I never return?
LANYON Do you think that likely?

Pause. He looks at her over the newspaper; sees that she is being serious.

Oh.

He puts down the newspaper.

I see.

Silence.

ELEANOR I'm sorry.
LANYON For what...?
ELEANOR For... never loving you the way you deserved.
LANYON Didn't you?
ELEANOR I think... I could have been a better wife...
LANYON I don't believe that. No-one has had a better wife than I have.

ELEANOR What I've put you through...

LANYON Eleanor, listen to me. I am not the best looking man; or indeed the most charming –

ELEANOR Hastie!

LANYON No, no, let me finish... nor am I the wittiest... and we both know I can't hold a candle to my peers professionally. But I have a good heart. It is the one thing I can be proud of. Big enough for you to dwell within it, whatever the mood or consequence. I don't regret a moment we have spent together; do you know that? Not one.

ELEANOR I don't know what to say.

LANYON There is no need to say anything. If you want to return to Ireland; be with your family... I understand.

ELEANOR I...

LANYON And if, over time, you think that you have found your natural place in the world, return to London and we will divorce. I will not contest it. Should you happen to miss me, on the other hand... I will always be here.

ELEANOR You should not be this good to me.

LANYON I don't know how else to be.

He smiles at her once again.

I will never close the door on you. Whatever we are to each other.

She nods.

Now, there is some money in the safe here; you will need it if you are going away for a while… I'll just… let me…

***LANYON** exits; crushed. **ELEANOR** creates the park bench, then stands behind it.*

ELEANOR *(To audience)* We made the same polite conversation as we always had on the way to Euston the following morning, and as the train heaved its way North, I wondered whether what Hastie had just shown me was braver, more noble; more incredible than any of Henry Jekyll's achievements.

***JEKYLL** enters. Sits.*

Hastie told me he would write frequently, and he did. Three times a week, at first… but then – in May of 1897 –

JEKYLL *(To audience)* May, 1897.

ELEANOR *(To audience)* The letters stopped…

***ELEANOR** exits. We hear birdsong.*

JEKYLL *(To audience)* Two months without incident, and I felt lighter and happier than ever. Yes, I was in pain physically, but my soul, for want of a clearer expression, was at peace. I had taken to walking out amongst my neighbours in the park across from my home, and sat one day, staring out at two children and their governess, wrestling with a bright red kite. It was a beautiful, late spring morning, and… I…

There is a pause; a momentary lack of focus. ***JEKYLL*** *shifts body position, giving an almost imperceptible shudder. His facial expression changes. He looks down at his hands. Lifts them up. Examines them with growing horror. He is* ***HYDE****.*

(As ***HYDE****)* …I felt exposed. Like a nerve. Eyes upon me. All knowing; everyone – and him in my head, screaming. *(Loud)* Don't tell me what to do!

A beat. Upstage, ***ELEANOR*** *and* ***UTTERSON*** *enter. Look at* ***HYDE****. Begin to whisper.*

People now; looking. The governess, the children. An old man with a dog. Does he know? Do they know…? They can't not know, can they? I have to get away, have to run. Where are you going? I see him ask; banging at the door in my mind. Banging at the glass. Where are you going? You'll be hunted; trapped. (Loud) Shut up! Shut up, if you want to live, shut up!

UTTERSON and ELEANOR stop whispering. UTTERSON blows a whistle.

A whistle? Whose whistle? A hand on my shoulder; the governess.

ELEANOR provides the voice of the GOVERNESS.

GOVERNESS Are you all right?

HYDE I hit her in the face and run. *(Loud)* How can I stop? It's my nature!

He moves downstage.

I hail a cab.

UTTERSON is the CABBIE.

CABBIE Where to?

HYDE He says. "Where to?" I want to slit his throat. *(Screaming)* Anywhere! He pulls the reins and we're off; I'm hidden. Calmer; need to think. I mumble the name of a hotel, and we're on our way. Got one dose of the formula left, but it's in the medical chambers in the cripple's cabinet.

A beat. The whispering has recommenced – now the words of ***JEKYLL*** *in* ***HYDE****'s head – "where are you going? You'll be hunted; trapped." It grows progressively louder.*

We reach the place. The cabbie looks at me; sidelong. Eyes squint. Does he know me? Know the reward on offer? I've got my collar up, hand over my face – I pay him way over the odds. My mind's screaming now, I can barely contain it. *(Bellowing)* Shut up!

Laughing, ***ELEANOR*** *and* ***UTTERSON*** *exit.*

Where do I turn? Can't get the formula – police will be watching the house. The lawyer will have given the letter over, I'm certain of that – I need rest, to stop the voice in my head... and I need someone I can trust...

LANYON *enters, reading a letter.*

Lanyon...

LANYON *(Reading)* Dear Lanyon, You are one of my oldest friends, and although we may have differed at times on scientific questions, I cannot remember any break in our affection.

HYDE *(To audience)* I get writing materials from the desk, and with the steadiest hand I can muster, I begin to write…

LANYON *(Reading)* Hastie, my life, my honour, my reason are all at your mercy; if you fail me tonight, I am lost.

HYDE *(To audience)* I keep it short, but precise – I can't afford for him to make any mistake…

LANYON *(Reading)* Take your carriage to my house as soon as you receive this letter. You will find Poole, my butler, waiting for you.

HYDE *(To audience)* …once I finish that letter, I write one to Poole… he needs to break into my chambers in the out-building…

***HYDE** rubs frantically at his face. He is struggling with concentration.*

LANYON *(Reading)* You are to enter my chambers alone, break open the cabinet to the left of the fireplace and take the contents of the fourth drawer down…

HYDE *(To audience)* I pay a commissionaire five shillings to deliver the notes; with the promise of a further five if he returns with receipt of delivery.

LANYON *(Reading)* You should be back long before midnight. At the stroke of twelve, be alone in your consulting room...

HYDE *(To audience)* After that, I wait until dusk...

LANYON *(Reading)* ...and admit with your own hand a man who will present himself in my name.

HYDE *(To audience)* ...and take another cab to Cavendish Square.

LANYON *(To audience)* Place in his hands the items you brought with you.

HYDE *(To audience)* I wait under the window and listen for the sound of the clock...

There is the sound of a clock chiming.

LANYON *(Reading)* Five minutes afterwards, if you insist upon an explanation, you will have understood that these arrangements are of capital importance, and that by the neglect of one of them, you might have charged your conscience with my death... or the shipwreck of my reason. Serve me, my dear Lanyon, and save your friend. H.J.

As the final note chimes, ***HYDE*** *and* ***LANYON*** *move together. Lights.*

(*To* ***HYDE***) Are you come from Dr. Jekyll?

HYDE *nods. He is agitated.*

Well, then.

HYDE Have you got it? Have you got it?

LANYON Come, sir; you forget that I have not yet the pleasure of your acquaintance. Please, sit. You must forgive my appearance; it's been a while since I had any company…

With barely-checked frustration, ***HYDE*** *sits.* ***LANYON*** *sits opposite. Smiles.*

Now…

HYDE I beg your pardon, Dr. Lanyon; I understand my manner must seem a little… odd; only, I'm here at the insistence of your colleague Dr. Jekyll, and I understood…

He pauses, forcing a hand against his brow; clearly ***JEKYLL*** *is screaming to get out.*

...I understood a flask...

***LANYON** removes a flask from one of the crates.*

LANYON Here it is.

***HYDE** snatches it from **LANYON** and backs away, looking at it, almost cradling it. He is grinding his jaw, shaking. He cannot get the lid off.*

Compose yourself, old boy.

***LANYON** takes it back and removes the lid himself. He hands it back to **HYDE,** who looks inside and smiles, before fixing **LANYON** with a stare.*

HYDE And now, to settle what remains. There is a choice before you. Think before you make it. I can leave this house now, and you will be neither richer nor wiser. Or, if curiosity has overtaken you, I shall remain, and a new province of knowledge; a new avenue to fame and power will be laid open to you.

***LANYON** smiles.*

LANYON I can see why you and Henry are friends; you sound just like him.

A beat.

It is late, and so I will not delay my answer. As tired as I am, I would rather see the end to this mystery before you depart.

HYDE Very well. Remember now; you made this choice.

LANYON I did.

***HYDE** starts to swirl the glass as he speaks. Music starts to play. The introduction to an Irish ballad. **ELEANOR** enters. Stands upstage.*

HYDE Remember, too, your oath – what follows is under the seal of our profession…

LANYON Are you a medical man too?

HYDE *(Ignoring his question)* …and is all, for the greater part, down to your intervention.

LANYON Mine?

HYDE You… who have so long been bound to the most narrow and material views…

LANYON I'm sorry?

HYDE …who have denied the virtue of transcendental medicine, who have derided and constrained your superiors… behold!

***HYDE** swallows the potion. **ELEANOR** begins to sing. Immediately **HYDE** begins to convulse, shake, groan…*

LANYON What's... (happening?)

LANYON *starts to see a change in* ***HYDE****. He starts to recognise* ***JEKYLL****.*

Oh God! No! No! I can't... no! What have you done? What have you done? Oh God! Oh God!

JEKYLL *stands before him.*

JEKYLL Hastie... it's me...

LANYON *is up; screaming, raging.*

LANYON Stay away! God; please! Stay away!

JEKYLL *moves towards him.*

Don't touch me... don't touch me!

LANYON *flees, screaming.* ***JEKYLL*** *breaks down in tears and flees. The verse finishes.*

ELEANOR *(To audience)* It had been a week since I had heard any news from England, then two items arrived in the post. I recognised the handwriting on one, a parcel from London. It was Henry's. There were instructions on the reverse to open it only in the event of his death. I set it to one side and opened the other; a letter from the lawyer, Gabriel Utterson…

UTTERSON *enters in black tie, an umbrella hoist.* ***ELEANOR*** *exits.*

UTTERSON *(To audience)* I was not surprised that Lanyon's widow did not attend the funeral. I wasn't sure my letter would reach her in time. His passing was so sudden; so unusual… I had seen him a week before he died, and it was almost as if he had given up on life.

A beat.

I stood amidst virtual strangers, listening to prayer combine with birdsong and early summer rainfall as they lowered his casket into the ground… and after the committal, I moved through the headstones to where my sister was interred. Poor Elizabeth; she had died in pain and anguish, her mind an… unfathomable… mess…

He breaks off as if something had caught his eye. ***HYDE*** *enters upstage.*

Hyde! Wreathed in the shadow of an ash tree, moving from foot to foot – small, nimble movements; a caged panther, he remained as the rest of the mourners departed...

***HYDE** heads downstage. Bends down to look at the grave. Considers.*

HYDE *(Quietly; almost to himself)* "Now if I do what I do not want to do, it is no longer I who do it."

UTTERSON I beg your pardon?

***HYDE** stands. Faces **UTTERSON**.*

HYDE "It is sin living within me that does it." Romans; chapter seven.

***UTTERSON** does not speak. **HYDE** turns to depart.*

UTTERSON A word with you, sir.

***HYDE** pauses momentarily; considers turning round, then continues upstage.*

Mr. Hyde, unless you wish for me to scream at the top of my lungs for the police, I suggest you stay and listen to what I have to say.

***HYDE** approaches **UTTERSON**. Gestures for him to speak.*

(Gesturing towards the grave) Who was this man to you?

***HYDE** shrugs.*

I ask again, sir –

HYDE I heard you the first time.

UTTERSON Then you will do me the honour of answering.

***HYDE** says nothing.*

Listen to me – you may have frightened Dr. Jekyll, but I don't scare so easily. I am not sure how you knew the deceased, but I'm certain the reason Jekyll isn't here to pay his respects is down to the fact that you are.

HYDE I cannot deny it.

UTTERSON You are not welcome; do you understand? You need to – (return to wherever it is you were hiding)

HYDE *(Forcefully)* Hastings Lanyon, born October 6th 1857, the only son of Charles and Jane. Charles was a mill owner, Jane a factory worker who caught his fancy. Their second child, a daughter, was stillborn. Hastie was an energetic boy; moved to London and studied medicine from 1879 to 1884. In life, respected, honest, industrious. Now? Nothing. A name on a slab that people will walk past and disregard. Food for worms, and not much of a feast at that.

A beat.

UTTERSON I… you… I ought to…

HYDE Ought? Oh aye, you "ought," but you never will, will you? That's the trouble with "ought." Ought never won any battles. Ought is now. It's everything about now.

***HYDE** squares up to **UTTERSON**.*

UTTERSON Who are you, Hyde?

HYDE I am a man free of doubt, regret; moral restraints… free of the world of "ought." I say what I mean, and I do what I say. Imagine being able to express yourself in that way. Imagine a world filled with people that could.

UTTERSON That's nothing short of pandemonium.

HYDE Is it?

UTTERSON Of course. It's chaos.

HYDE Then chaos is coming.

UTTERSON From where?

HYDE Everywhere! You're so blind; look; listen – they're out there. There is a huge, seething mass of people waking up every day with a gnawing feeling in their gut, knowing there's something else, there's something more, there's something they want. When it starts, it won't be about politics; it will be about greed. Because eventually the masses will realise that they don't have to kowtow, tug their forelocks, bow and scrape to get what they need. They can cheat. They can lie. And they'll be no worse thought of on this earth. Oh, they're out there, John – they're growing in number. They'll never stop.

UTTERSON Behaviour like yours can't sustain! Society won't stand for it.

HYDE Society? Society will be built on it. By it. A hundred years from now, do you think there'll be more of you on the earth… or more of me?

UTTERSON You're insane.

HYDE I'm not insane. I'm the future. And deep down, you know it.

***UTTERSON** exits. **HYDE** takes beakers, pipettes and other scientific equipment from one of the crates. Places them on the table. Talks as he is measuring things into Petri dishes and so on.*

(To audience) Six days, the final dose lasted. And now I'm out for good – no doctor's body to hide in; save me from the noose. Visiting Lanyon's grave wasn't wise, but I had to go... the cripple wouldn't leave me alone; the headaches, the lack of sleep, the attempts to get this right...

With a sweep of his arm, it is on the floor. He holds his head in frustration...

Coming back, I leave notes by the door to the chamber, sending the servants out to get raw materials. I make up batch after batch of the formula... but nothing is working. Or maybe I wasn't... smart enough; maybe the cripple wouldn't let me share that part of his brain... *(Shouting)* Shut up! Shut up!

There is a knocking.

(Calling off) Who is it?

BRADSHAW It's Miss Bradshaw, sir.
HYDE If it's another delivery, leave it outside.
BRADSHAW It's a cheque, sir. Mr. Poole opened it.
HYDE A cheque?

BRADSHAW From Hook & Sons in Greenwich. A refund, I think. And a letter.

He reaches into a crate and pulls on the mask, then reaches for the cane.

HYDE Come in and bring it to me.

***BRADSHAW** enters. She is terrified enough, but as soon as she sees the satanic face, she is beside herself.*

Set it down on the table there.

She does so; almost in tears. Manages the ghost of a curtsey and hightails it out, exiting with a kind of wail. ***HYDE** opens the letter. The cheque he sets aside. He reads, and howls with anguish.*

No! No!

He screws it up. Laughs bitterly.

(To audience) The first compound... the one that worked... that this, all this came from... was tainted with "unknown variants." Unknown; unknowable... God! And there; the sum total of my life's worth – one pound, eighteen shillings and ninepence.

He screams.

July 1897. I've worked on every supplier, run up debts, and I can't draw on any money because I burnt the chequebooks... he's going... my hiding place; the voice in my head... the only man who holds the key to finding these unknown variants... I hear him less distinctly, it's more now... more a buzzing; buzzing, like black wasps in my skull, black wasps... can't sleep... and nothing is working!

Music. ***HYDE*** *picks up the equipment; looks over the equations on the wall and tries to start over.* ***UTTERSON*** *enters with* ***ELEANOR*** *as* ***BRADSHAW****. They cross the back.*

UTTERSON Do you know what time it is, girl?

BRADSHAW I know sir, but Mr. Poole sent me; he says you've got to come.

UTTERSON What's happened?

BRADSHAW He thinks the villain's back, sir. He's locked himself in the outbuildings... crying day and night; he doesn't sound anything like the master.

UTTERSON Indeed.

BRADSHAW Sir, Mr. Poole thinks he's done the Doctor in!

*They exit. **HYDE** screams.*

HYDE *(To audience)* Everything I drink, however vast the quantity, however much I vomit, however long I pass out for, I'm still me when I awake. I go back to the formula before last; it made me sick blood, but maybe if I try something else with it; a control substance, or…

There is a hammering, as if on a door.

UTTERSON *(Off)* Dr. Jekyll? Are you in there?

***HYDE** looks round in blind panic.*

HYDE Go away!

UTTERSON *(Off)* Harry, you have to let me in. Your staff are terrified; they think the fiend is back.

HYDE Tell them all to go! Go!

UTTERSON *(Off)* I have a locksmith here. He'll have no choice but to open the door for me unless you do…

HYDE Don't… please… please…

UTTERSON *(Off)* I'm sorry; I have no choice.

*There is the sound of thumping outside. **JEKYLL** looks at the phial in his hand.*

HYDE *(To audience)* I'm undone. Banging at the door, banging in my head, and what can I do? What can I do...? I can't face the gallows... I can't...

He collapses to the floor, sobbing. Then pulls himself together, returns to the crate and brings out a jar of brown liquid, clearly labelled poison. He drinks it. ***ELEANOR*** *enters, singing.*

Strange; my last thoughts are of her. I wonder what the song she sang in the second half of the show was like? I wonder if she knew I loved her as much as I hated myself? And I wonder...

He is caught mid-sentence by the poison, and with the briefest of choking noises, collapses onto the floor. The banging gets louder, as does he music, and with one final crash, ***UTTERSON*** *enters to find* ***HYDE****'s stricken body. He cradles it momentarily. Lights fade on* ***HYDE*** *and* ***UTTERSON****, and down to a spotlight on* ***ELEANOR****.* ***UTTERSON*** *and* ***HYDE*** *exit. At the end of* ***ELEANOR****'s song, we hear a recording of applause. She exits as* ***UTTERSON*** *enters.*

UTTERSON *(To audience)* Dr. Jekyll died on July 11th, 1897. His funeral was understated; the reading of his Will, frankly, embarrassing. It would appear that on or around the date of Lanyon's passing,

Harry had made a final amendment, bequeathing everything, the house, grounds, fortune... to me. I had also been left a letter, explaining the whole sorry business... that, along with a letter left me by Hastie Lanyon, was very much the end of the case of Dr. Jekyll and Mr. Hyde... but only the start for me.

A beat.

At four o'clock in the afternoon of August 4th, 1897, I was in this room, gathering my thoughts as much as anything. My friend's chambers, where I saw what remained of... him... breathe his last. In truth I had not even begun to consider what to do with the property, the staff... and I was simply contemplating a picture positioned behind Harry's desk, when –

There is the sound of knocking.

(Calling) Come.

Nothing. Another knock.

Poole? We're beyond formalities; come in, man!

ELEANOR *(Off)* I'm not a man.

***ELEANOR** enters, carrying a leather document case. She moves awkwardly to **UTTERSON**. She is pregnant.*

Your man there; he said I should…

***UTTERSON** smiles politely. Gestures for **ELEANOR** to sit.*

UTTERSON How long have you been back?

ELEANOR Three days. Took my old lodgings in Spitalfields, near the music hall where I first met…

UTTERSON Hastie.

ELEANOR Yes. Yes.

UTTERSON You didn't return to Cavendish Square…?

***ELEANOR** shakes her head.*

The house there is yours. He willed it to you.

ELEANOR I can't. Not after…

UTTERSON Anything that happened between you and Henry Jekyll is none of my concern.

ELEANOR Thank you, Gabriel.

UTTERSON If you would prefer I can arrange to have it sold…

ELEANOR That's not why I'm here.

Pause. She looks around.

So, this…?

UTTERSON I'm not sure what to do. I've had a housemaid, you understand; never a house full of the beggars.

ELEANOR You'll get used to it.

UTTERSON I don't know as I want to.

A beat.

ELEANOR I loved him, Gabriel. You know? Really… really loved him. Vividly. You probably can't understand that; me being a married woman, and…

UTTERSON It's not my place to judge.

***ELEANOR** smiles.*

ELEANOR Can I ask –

A beat.

When he died…

UTTERSON Yes?

ELEANOR Were you there?

***UTTERSON** nods.*

Who was he?

UTTERSON I'm sorry?

ELEANOR When he died...? Who was he when he died?

UTTERSON Who? I don't follow...

ELEANOR Yes you do.

A beat.

UTTERSON My good God. You knew?

***ELEANOR** nods.*

For how long?

ELEANOR Does it matter?

She takes an envelope from inside the case.

This is for you.

***UTTERSON** takes the letter. Sits and opens it. Light upstage; **JEKYLL** appears.*

JEKYLL John. What you have before you is everything I have come to understand about the human mind. My part in the experiment is over, but my work must go on. I am entrusting you with this because I know that this is real for you. Find a man with skill; have him continue where I left off. I was closer than anyone has yet come to the mysteries of the psyche – for humanity's sake and Elizabeth's memory I urge you to take that next step. Your friend. Harry.

*Light out. **JEKYLL** remains. Silence. **ELEANOR** holds out the leather case.*

ELEANOR Here. It's all inside.

UTTERSON I can't accept that.

ELEANOR You have to.

A beat.

He said you wouldn't understand.

UTTERSON Not understand? He became a monster! He killed! Your husband, amongst others!

ELEANOR There is more at stake here.

UTTERSON No! There is murder, and chaos and… no good can come of this.

ELEANOR You know, Henry took me to a hospital on the Sussex coast once. A run down little place, with grounds overlooking the sea. We were there to visit your sister.

UTTERSON Do not make this about her.

ELEANOR I saw the way she was treated.

UTTERSON And what? It would be better that people like her…

ELEANOR He just needed more time; different subjects – self-testing was a mistake; read the notes!

UTTERSON I don't need to read the notes. What I need to do is burn them.

ELEANOR Please. Please. He came this close to a full understanding of the human mind – with no surgery, no torture – and with that kind of understanding comes a direct pathway – (to curing one of the sicknesses of our age)

UTTERSON God, you do sound like him.

A beat.

Eleanor, I cannot condone a course of action that would lead to suffering…

ELEANOR He's not asking for that. He's asking you to do the right thing. The potential you hold in your hands… given to the right man…

UTTERSON And who would that be? I wouldn't even begin to know how to look for a successor.

ELEANOR Then you employ someone who works in medicine, to watch the colleges… find a capable, driven student. Someone like Henry.

UTTERSON What if I choose the wrong subject? What if they get it wrong?

ELEANOR What if they don't?

A beat.

History will forgive you, Gabriel. It will even forget you.

UTTERSON I… I'm not… (the man for this task)

ELEANOR Henry is asking for your help.

UTTERSON He would understand my reluctance. I urge you to do the same.

ELEANOR Think of Elizabeth then. What might she want?

UTTERSON My sister is dead. I loved her, but she died.

ELEANOR Then do it for me. And for…

***ELEANOR** wordlessly touches her stomach. Pause.*

UTTERSON How long?

ELEANOR Five and a half months.

UTTERSON And its Lanyon's?

ELEANOR No.

UTTERSON Jekyll's, then?

*She shakes her head; starts to cry. In the half-light at the back of the stage, **JEKYLL** slowly transforms into the body position of **HYDE. UTTERSON** realises what that can mean.*

Oh God. Oh Jesus Christ.

Music starts to play; a reprise of Danse Macabre. ***HYDE*** *slowly pulls the mask over his face once again.*

ELEANOR Please, Gabriel. Please. Do what's right. Do what's right.

She kisses him briefly on the cheek, and exits. ***UTTERSON*** *is left alone.* ***HYDE*** *laughs softly at the back of the stage, as* ***UTTERSON*** *sinks into a chair and reaches into the nearest crate, pulling out a whisky bottle. He takes a drink directly from it, then picks up the research from the table. He opens the folder and starts leafing through it as* ***HYDE*** *looks over his shoulder, then up at the audience as the music swells and the lights fade.*

The End

Much thanks in the writing of this adaptation are due to a number of good friends, who also happen to have studied science to a high level. First and foremost, Dr. Lorraine Earps, whose knowledge of the history of neuroscience was an incredible, invaluable help... as was Dr. Darren Haggerston, who, along with assisting in the discussions, also kept my Godson Jamie occupied whilst I talked things through with Lorrie. Graham Leech, too, gave me some fantastic advice on the different areas of the brain which fed into the play perfectly. Thanks for all your help – I am in your debt. NL.